W9-BKT-944

C.NORTHCOTE PARKINSON

BIG BUSINESS

LITTLE, BROWN AND COMPANY BOSTON TORONTO

ISBN 0 297 76780 1

Library of Congress Catalog Card No. 74-3642

Printed in Great Britain

Frontispiece: the headquarters of the Bank of
America, in San Francisco.

CONTENTS

BOARD
GAMES

1 THE PUBLIC IMAGE

Far above the ordinary haunts of men, on the topmost floor of the highest-rise building in the biggest city's busiest quarter, is the office of the wealthiest company's chief executive. We may never glimpse it, that innermost sanctum, but we know its appearance, its atmosphere, its meaning. It is furnished with costly simplicity (here a Hogarth, there a Matisse) and defended by successive offices and doors. The great man, we realize, is not readily accessible. Middle-aged, distinguished, grey-haired but bronzed, he is briefly glimpsed between his car and the entrance and again between the entrance and his car. From motion pictures and from television we derive our picture of his day's activity. We realize, for instance, that his desk will be tidy, little of its surface being hidden by paper. His predecessor of an earlier age would have had six telephones in simultaneous use, three secretaries at his elbow and a dozen executives entering and leaving by as many doors. But that scene is evidently outmoded, today's captain of industry being as often in conference as on the telephone. Such, however, is our televisual education that we can imagine the dialogue as readily as we can picture the scene:

'Get me Mr Vandeputt, please, of Amsterdam. Put Lord Rochester through in the meanwhile. That you, Neville? John here. The answer is "no". Our offer of nine million stands, but we won't at present go higher. What's that? But *our* computer tells a different story. Call me again if you have second thoughts. Not tomorrow, though, as I shall be in Vancouver. Goodbye! . . . Ah, Miss Swift, are you through to Amsterdam? Good. Mr Vandeputt? John Durant here. Your terms are agreed except on one minor point. The contract is on its way to you, giving us a controlling interest. The group, as thus enlarged, will have virtual control of the market. You will realize that some of our smaller competitors will have to disappear. I look forward to having you on the board. Goodbye.'

The great man touches a key on his desk and his secretary appears as if by magic.

'Show the others in, Miss Seymour.'

Four key executives file in and take their places at a hexagonal table. Miss Seymour takes the sixth place and notes each decision as it is reached. The discussion is too allusive and technical to mean anything to an eavesdropper, were such a person (unbelievably) present. An eye must be kept on the government's anti-pollution committee with a view to possible action at a later stage. Project thirty-two is now ready for submission to the board. Two and a half million will go to the reserve fund. The labour force at plant Z will be reduced by three hundred. As from September more will be done to advertise product G. There remains the question about Lagging, the plant manager at Y. 'Best fire him at once. Agreed?' (all nod). 'Make an appointment for him to see me on Monday, Miss Seymour. Any more business? Thank you, gentlemen. Next week, then.'

The conference ends and the great man turns again to his secretary:

'I must be on my way to the airport. Should Mr Roebuck call during

'I'm a busy man – what can I do for you?'
A cartoonist's view of management.

the next thirty minutes, put him through to the car. Should Mr Harding call from the Treasury, put him through to Mr Levitt. Make my excuses to the French Ambassador about Friday's reception. Tell anyone else who matters that I'll be back tomorrow afternoon from three. Goodbye till then.'

The chief executive has gone like a whirlwind, and all who are left relax for a moment, shrinking to human size. Miles away already,

One of the languages of big business: stocks and shares.

an expensive chauffeur-driven car is weaving its way through the city traffic while the chief's personal assistant is calling the office and simultaneously jotting down on a pad the further dates which have to be arranged. 'I'll interview Mr Rising on Tuesday. Make a memo to ask him ... Wait, though. Take that call on the other line. Mr Roebuck? Yes ... yes ... I see. Call me again, will you? I shall need to think it over. Right . . . that memo now. Who did Rising marry and when? Find out, please.' The car speeds on its way and we are left to stare after it in wild surmise. How can so vast an organization be run with such smooth competence?

Our idea of big business might be fairly summarized in a scene such as that. It could be altered, of course, to suit the preconception of the reader. Were the scene re-written, however, in terms of ecstatic veneration, or in terms of virulent abuse, the essential elements would have to be the same. We all grasp that the organization concerned must be of great size, with numerous plants or distribution centres, and with not fewer than ten thousand people on the payroll. It must operate on a vast scale of investment and expenditure. Its interests must ramify throughout a continent and indeed across the world. To achieve this there must be rapid means of communication – the telephone, the aeroplane, the railway and the car. Without these aids the central direction of a widespread empire would not be technically possible. But behind that centralized control there lurks a single-minded and ruthless purpose. The corporation has an aim which is purely economic. Its success is measured only in terms of finance. Its language, and the language of all business, is money.

Big business in modern times was the invention of Cornelius Vanderbilt (1794–1877) who made his fortune out of US railroads. By the time he died he was the richest man in the USA, leaving $105 million to his son, who doubled that fortune to become the richest man in the world. Since that time big business has always been regarded as a typically American phenomenon. This may not be entirely true, but millionaires in the USA have enjoyed a sort of eminence which is denied them in countries where the chess board is already occupied by kings, queens, bishops and knights. Given the steamship from about 1840, the railway from about 1850 and the telegraph from about 1860, the new type of business man came into existence. He was exposed from the start to both adulation and attack.

To understand the millionaire's public image and the subsequent

Cornelius Vanderbilt, the railway and shipping magnate who became the richest man in the USA, is regarded by many as the founder of big business.

image of the giant organization he founded, we have to realize that his rise to prominence coincided with the rise of what we call representative democracy. In earlier periods of history a man of wealth – his fortune gained more often from banking or commerce than from industry – was absorbed fairly readily into an existing society. There might be some hint of rejection, some mutterings about the bad manners of the parvenu, but the opposition was actually shortlived. One or two judicious marriages were enough to secure election to the club, enabling the upstart to convert wealth into social status and political power.

Democracy dawned in the USA during the presidency of Andrew Jackson (1829–37), one effect being to create the professional politician, the man who talks his way into office. As from that time in the USA, and from a rather later period in Britain, the man of wealth was progressively excluded from office by the man of words. There were instances of millionaires having the gift of eloquence, but wealth could also be a handicap in popular appeal and the millionaire's traits – tenacity, foresight, energy and ruthlessness – were often accompanied by reticence, shyness and contempt for the mob.

The familiar picture was of the industrialist excluded from political office but able to bribe the penniless politician. So the public image of the millionaire was unfavourable from the beginning. He was seen to show no concern for the public welfare. His motives were purely economic and he was lacking even in patriotism. He was capable of selling munitions to the country's potential enemies. He was equally capable of selling defective ammunition to his own side. He cared nothing for the great political issues and less than nothing for the sufferings of the poor. His sole concern was to make money, paying the lowest wages which anyone would accept and charging the highest prices that anyone would pay. If he spent his money on riotous living he added to the misery of the poor by pointing the contrast between their lives and his. If he hoarded his money he was withholding employment. If he left his fortune to his children they would be written off as parasites.

However, he held no public office, so it was impossible to vote against him. But the mere fact of his wealth was enough to suggest that he must have influence. Politicians – and especially local politicians – began as relatively poor men, basing their appeal on their first-hand knowledge of how the poor lived. But were they proof against bribery? How would their inevitable relationship with the business men of their community develop? There was always the possibility of corruption lying behind the unknown factors.

We know very little about big business. Perhaps this is natural. A hundred years ago it was possible for one brilliant man to master all that was known of the science of chemistry. Today this would be unthinkable. Indeed, any small branch could occupy the lifetimes of a score of brilliant scientists. So it is with the science of business. The multitude of affairs, from finance to market research, from computers to advertising, from product design to systems analysis – each requires the attention of experts. And, as we know only too well, the expert is not readily understood except by his own kind.

Big business is the product of several forces. In the first place it is our employer. We also know it as a producer. We know the stories of successes and failures as they are reflected in the lives of the great industrial adventurers. And we know big business as a force in itself, an ever-enlarging entity, growing by internal expansion, or by absorption and merger. And, deep down, most of us fear big business.

When, in 1932, a study[1] of US industrial concentration predicted that, given the existing trends, the top two hundred companies would account for virtually all industrial output within thirty years, this caused little rejoicing. On the contrary, it sparked off a further round of attacks on big business, and spurred the US Government to further action to curb monopolies. For the public image of big business has rarely been favourable. Big business, certainly, is a fact of life. Yet it is a fact which society has not found easy to accept. Since the latter part of the nineteenth century, when huge business corporations first began to make their mark on the public, a mixture of hostility and adulation has coloured the attitudes of society.

A glance at the names of the giant corporations shows that most of them are to be found in the USA. This was always so. From the heroic days of Rockefeller and Carnegie until the present age of General Motors and Chrysler, the mammoths have made their home in the USA. And because the USA saw the earliest and most vigorous flourishing of these giants, public attitudes there have been more extreme than elsewhere. As long ago as 1890, legislation was passed by Congress to check the threat presented by big business. That act is still on the statute books, and US big business is still big. In Britain, Germany, France, Australia, Japan – indeed in all the industrial nations of the non-communist world – huge enterprises

LE PATRON a besoin de toi

tu n'as pas besoin de lui

are a powerful social and economic force. Moreover, through the spread of subsidiaries, there is no nation in the capitalist world which is outside their orbit.

Menace or mirage? To judge by public opinion over the decades, the dangers of big business seem only too real. Not only has it endured attacks from many quarters, from governments, courts, economists, historians, newspapers and novelists, but also there are many instances of ruthlessness, fraud and intrigue in the building-up and conduct of giant corporations.

Anti-business bias has complex roots. In part, big business shares the stigma sometimes attached to all business. Dark satanic mills replace the weaver's cottage; droning machinery, with its discipline and routine, vanquishes the individual skills of the craftsman. And the urge of the industrialist to make profits is frequently seen as unwholesome by people who seldom stop to think that the farmer and the artisan are driven by the same motives.

Sheer size is frightening, and big corporations inspire awe and fear. It is, of course, instinctive in human nature to support the weak against the strong. Giant business concerns seem predatory, for they grow at the expense of little concerns and acquire a momentum of their own. Above all, they are wealthy. Their assets are counted in tens of millions, their decisions involve the disposition of fortunes far beyond those carried in the richest Spanish treasure ship. Wealth brings power, and power fosters fear among outsiders. Individuals have no redress against the power of big business. The public has had to turn to governments to check and curtail the power of the modern corporation.

Paradoxically, big businesses are also feared because so little is known about them. The larger corporations become, the more they disappear into the shadows. Brand names are household words, but the figures behind those brands seem remote, even sinister. For today, corporations have far outgrown the conceptions of even their most ambitious and imaginative founders. Individual or family ownership of large firms is a thing of the past. Huge corporations make decisions affecting the lives of millions, affecting even the prosperity of the nation. Yet the public does not know who makes these decisions. The anonymity of big business, the image of 'faceless men' controlling untold wealth and manipulating the activities of a nation – these are part of the public idea of the modern corporation.

The public does not understand big business. Forces that generate huge corporations and make them grow ever larger can only be seen

OPPOSITE *'The employer needs you, you don't need him.'* A French communist poster which appeared during the Paris riots of May 1968.

in terms of some devouring monster. Remote, complex, mechanical, inexorable, the huge enterprise seems to exist independently of the men who ostensibly control it.

John Kenneth Galbraith has written about the role of big corporations in modern society.[2] According to him, the sovereignty of the consumer has given way to the sovereignty of the corporation. No longer do firms produce what consumers demand. The imperatives of large-scale enterprise, and the vast accumulations of capital required by modern production and technology, determine that firms decide what and how much should be produced. The consumer passively takes the end product. Galbraith himself does not explicitly condemn these activities; he views them as an inevitable consequence of modern technology, and records them rather as a medieval stoic might record the plague. Yet such a picture of the behaviour of business firms and business men is an expression of the fears felt perhaps by all of us.

In other ways, too, large corporations seem at war with society. Business brings pollution, big business brings big pollution. Unsightly factories and office blocks spoil countryside and urban skyline. Industry fights with country lovers for open spaces. Some of the world's greatest natural assets are threatened by exploitation by giant firms. And industry produces effluent that poisons and discolours rivers and pollutes the atmosphere. A large part of present-day concern with the eroding natural environment is connected with the activities of big business.

Rarely has the business man been depicted as a hero by those most influential in forming public opinion. In literature, the values of commerce have often been contrasted with the values of gentility and charity; among social historians the evils of factory masters and the amorality of the industrial manipulators have received more emphasis than the romance of enterprise; and among economists the terms 'monopoly' and 'oligopoly' imply a criticism which suggests more than just 'healthy competition'. Indeed, the word 'enterprise' suggests initiative, daring and imagination. Put the adjectives 'large', 'corporate' in front and very different connotations appear: something unwieldy, parasitic and predatory comes to mind.

As the industrial revolution took place in Britain, in the USA and Western Europe and by the close of the nineteenth century, in Russia and Japan, hostility to business grew. The Victorian romantics, Carlyle, Ruskin and Dickens, ranted against the values of an industrial society. In Russia, Chekhov's *Cherry Orchard* similarly emphasized the coarseness and harshness of middle-class conduct. Later, Arnold Bennett, Priestley, Orwell, and many others continued to denounce the abuses of industrialism. In the USA too, novels began to reflect the anti-business spirit of the times. The sordid commercial activities of a Chicago tycoon of the 1890s were described in Theodore Dreiser's trilogy, *The Financier*, *The Titan* and *The Stoic*. Upton Sinclair's *The Jungle* exposed the horrors of the Chicago meat packing industry in the early twentieth century, while Dos Passos and John Steinbeck added to the attacks on business practices which increased after the First World War.

The American stories about politicians as puppets of the wealthy are very numerous indeed, but possibly reach their dramatic peak in the motion pictures *Mr Deeds Comes to Town* and *Citizen Kane*. The chief character in the latter and more satiric film was based on that of William Randolph Hearst (1863–1951), a man of wealth and influence who was not himself in public office. When the same type of satire spread to Britain it was effectively used by Hilaire Belloc (1870–1953), who wrote a number of novels in which political corruption was described and presented as a common assumption. The plot of *A Change in the Cabinet* (1909) illustrates the invasion of the House of Lords by the newly rich.

From 1912 onwards there followed a series of rather similar novels, G. K. Chesterton's important amongst them. These books continued to appear at regular intervals until 1936, all showing the impact of big business on a more or less democratic form of government. Their effect, as intended, was disquieting.

A different picture came from H. G. Wells, whose Uncle Ponderovo in *Tono Bungay* owes his sudden wealth to energy and impudence. The uncle and nephew market a worthless patent medicine ('Tono Bungay') which contains, by their account, the secret of health, beauty and strength:

It was a game, an absurd but absurdly interesting game and the points were scored in cases of bottles. People think a happy notion is enough to make a man rich, that fortunes can be made without toil. It's a dream, as every millionaire (except one or two lucky gamblers) can testify. I doubt if J. D. Rockefeller in the early days of Standard Oil worked harder than we did.

Their medicine is a great success and Uncle Ponderovo points out what success can mean in Britain:

It's a wonderful system – this old British system, George. It's staid and stable, and yet it has a place for new men. We come up and take our places. It's almost expected. We take a hand. That's where our democracy differs from America. Over there a man succeeds; all he gets is money. Here there's a system – open to everyone – practically . . .

This was of course true. Wealthy and powerful men could be admitted to the House of Lords and so absorbed into the higher ranks of a well-established society.

In contrast with Belloc and Wells, Rudyard Kipling provides us, in *Captain Courageous* (1894), with a portrait of a US railway magnate which is far more sympathetic. Mr Cheyne has risen the hard way, coming to wealth after a life of tough adventure. If utterly ruined and left penniless he would probably be able to do it again. This is, however, an isolated picture. George Bernard Shaw presents a far more familiar one in *The Millionairess*:

What is to be done with that section of the possessors of specific talent whose talent is for moneymaking? History and daily experience teach us that if the world does not devise some plan of ruling them, they will rule the world. Now it is not desirable that they should rule the world; for the secret of moneymaking is to care for nothing else and to work at nothing else; and as the world's welfare depends on operations by which no individual can make money, whilst its ruin by war and drink and disease and drugs and debauchery is enormously profitable to moneymakers, the supremacy of the moneymaker is the destruction of the state. A society which depends on the incentive of private property is doomed.

The problem of the millionaire in a democratic society remains a problem except in so far as the millionaires can solve it for themselves.

Business has received little more sympathy at the hands of historians. Once the early flush of enthusiasm for the marvels of modern industry had died during the early nineteenth century, a far more critical, questioning attitude set in. The enthusiasm of George Porter's *Progress of a Nation*, and the adulation of Samuel Smiles' *Lives of the Engineers*, gave way to the disillusion of radical social historians like Charles Beard, William Prescott, Henry Adams and Charles Adams. All these were strongly biased against the values and practices of business. Charles Adams was somewhat exceptional in that he actually became a successful business man, reaching ultimately the chairmanship of the huge Union Pacific Railroad Company. He

wrote of his business colleagues, 'a less interesting crowd I do not care to encounter. Not one that I have ever known would I care to meet again, either in this world or the next; nor is one of them associated in my mind with the idea of humour, thought, or refinement.' At the very end of the century, Thorstein Veblen castigated the values of US capitalism. Veblen, more than any writer except Marx, shaped the modern intellectual attack against big business. His *Theory of the Leisure Class* made a sharp distinction between industry – the productive process of making goods, and business – the anti-social pursuit of profits. The Darwinian urge in man to compete with

A photograph taken *c.* 1880 inside the factory of Krupps, the famous arms manufacturers.

others and establish his personal superiority and dominance was reflected in the behaviour and ideals of business. Business was but the manifestation of a perverted side of man's nature.

As we have seen, reaction and hostility to big business came soonest in the USA. The Sherman Anti-Trust Act of 1890 was passed, ironically, just a few years before the largest, most outrageous, and most uncontrolled burst of giant corporate growth in the nation's history. This was the age of the 'robber barons'. 'Nothing is lost save honour,' as one of the most notorious of them, Jim Fisk, once said. By the first decade of the twentieth century, the clamour against big business reached a crescendo. 'Muckraking' started everywhere. The nation's most widely read magazines carried story after story of the frauds, crimes and corruption of big business. Fact blurred into fiction. Even a scholarly work such as Ida Tarbell's *History of the Standard Oil Company* dwelt heavily on the ruthlessness of Rockefeller as he set out to crush his competitors and build the greatest oil enterprise in the world.

Academic economists have seldom been among the admirers of big business. Orthodox, classical theory rests on an idealized state of 'perfect competition', where many firms compete with each other, and where prices are driven to their lowest point, enabling firms to cover cost and make a 'normal' but not excessive profit. The consumer obviously benefits from low prices and a wide choice of products from vigorously competing firms. Deviations from this situation, where one firm can make an abnormal profit by charging high prices or by restricting supply without fear of competition are against the public interest. Terms of abuse have been coined by economists to describe such situations – 'imperfect competition', 'perfect monopoly', where one firm is the sole producer of a commodity, and 'oligopoly', where a few large firms control the market, and are presumably in anti-social collusion.

Criticism of big business was rampant in 1900–10 but was stifled abruptly by the First World War. Governments which had legislated against monopoly were suddenly converted to the need for concentration. Under wartime conditions it was practically convenient to deal with each industry as a whole. Co-ordination was vital to transport and munitions and the large firms, being fewer, were easier to co-ordinate. Central to the war effort were the supplies of oil and steel, both already organized in gigantic combines. Captains of industry who had been accused of anti-social collusion were now brought into committees under government chairmanship. On the need for co-ordination there was an unwonted agreement between the fighting services and the believers in socialism. The generals and admirals wanted a centralized system of control, the socialists wanted the same thing but saw it as the first step towards nationalization.

It was often the wartime committee which unknowingly prepared the way for the post-war merger. Nor could the captains of industry be attacked in wartime for competing unfairly with their rivals. The utmost expansion of their business was merely a part of the war effort. They too were heroes in their way, as they were themselves the first to admit. For the period of the war and for some prosperous years afterwards they basked in the sunshine of an unusual popularity.

The image presented by the giant corporation is by no means wholly tarnished; nor, even in the USA, has hostility always prevailed. Prosperity has usually helped the large corporation; depression has brought disillusion and opposition. No clearer instance exists than in the USA after the First World War. This was a golden era of boom, confidence in the ability of US industry to lead the nation to permanent prosperity. Americans believed in big business. Their faith was reflected in many things, none more so than in the success of Bruce Barton's book *The Man Nobody Knows*. For two successive years in the twenties this was the best-selling non-fiction book in the USA. It was about Christianity, and he sold religion to Americans by showing them its resemblance to big business. Jesus was not simply 'the most popular dinner guest in Jerusalem,' but one of the 'top executives' of all time. 'He picked up twelve men from the bottom ranks of business and forged them into an organization that conquered the world. . . . Nowhere is there such a startling example of executive success as the way in which that organization was brought together.' His parables were 'the most powerful advertisements of all time,' and Jesus was, in fact, 'the founder of modern business'.

After this period of prosperity came the great crash of 1929 and the bitter, world-wide depression which followed. The standing of the business world collapsed. Capitalism, it seemed to many, had failed. Hardly surprising were the numerous frauds and commercial malpractices exposed in the ruins of the world's shattered economies. Hardly surprising also were the renewed efforts of governments to control the giant monopolies. When the Second World War ended, public hostility to big business had scarcely abated. To an already strong mistrust of the economic practices of large-scale industry

The giant firm of Krupps remained in the hands of the Krupp family, despite two world wars, until 1967.

RIGHT Herr Krupp, the inventor of the Krupp gun. BELOW Krupps in 1912.

LEFT A portrait of the
Krupp family.

was added the widespread conviction that big business in the Axis powers bore a grave political responsibility for the war. Allied governments were determined never again to permit the emergence of such huge armaments works as Krupp in Germany, or of the giant Japanese combines like Mitsubishi.

In the USA the Second World War had provided unwittingly a cloak for the development of big business:

The major contribution of big business to national security was un-disputed. But wartime requirements also contributed to a marked increase in the scale of big business. Of the eighteen billion dollars' worth of war plants constructed between 1940 and the end of 1943, nearly three-quarters were in units exceeding ten million dollars, and almost one-third in units above fifty million. In addition, some fifteen billion dollars' worth of war plants had been built and operated for the government by large private companies. Approximately seven-and-a-half billion dollars of government plant contracts were placed with thirty-one corporations, averaging over two hundred million per corporation. The great bulk of prime contracts went to the larger companies ... these developments implied that the disparity between big business and the rest of the economic structure had been accentuated by the wartime experience.[3]

Slowly, however, as economic recovery set in after the war, public opinion altered. Since about 1950 big business has once again found, if not favour, at least a more ready acceptance. Shifts in public opinion are never easy to pinpoint or explain. One reason for the growing tolerance must surely be the unparalleled prosperity and the full employment which has come to most big industrial countries since the early 1950s. As in the USA after the First World War, wealth has softened discontent. Above all, the nature and role of big business is changing, and in many ways this has improved its public image. Gradually and subtly big business has come to assume a mantle – many would still say a cloak – of social responsibility.

Many factors have brought about this change. Since the Second World War, governments in nearly all Western countries have played an increasingly active part in the direction of economic activity. They have, for example, attempted to regulate employment, prices and the rate of economic growth. To achieve such control they have been obliged to call on the leaders of industry (and the trade unions) to co-operate in their policies, and this in turn has given an aura of respectability to these leaders. In Britain, for example, it is

OPPOSITE Henry Ford I (1863–1947), one of the most remarkable names in the history of big business, and who, like so many others of the great names, gave much of his money to charity.

common for top industrial figures to feature in honours lists, and numerous heads of the major corporations are knights and peers of the realm. Moreover the increasingly vast public sector, with its huge nationalized industries, has made frequent raids on the capitalist domain to get successful leaders for itself.

Governments, whether they like it or not, depend on big business. They depend on it to carry through their defence policies successfully, for only the largest corporations have the resources of capital and technology to bring off an endeavour like the US space programme. And similarly a government-backed project like Concorde must have behind it the co-operation of giant corporations. Moreover the growth targets of governments depend on industrial prosperity and the export achievements of great industries. The British Government watches anxiously the fortunes of British Leyland, for example, and the national press reports the introduction of a new car model as an event of national significance.

More subtle factors have influenced the public's reaction to big business. The large firms are, generally speaking, good employers. Conditions of service, holidays, pension schemes, subsidized canteens, cheap housing loans: these and other 'benefits' have gone a long way towards reducing the inherent antagonism between employer and employee. And the names of the great leaders no longer mean rapacity and greed. Nobel, Rockefeller, Carnegie, Ford and Nuffield have left charitable foundations and are thus givers as well as takers.

Above all, the early fears about big business have not been realized. Far from dominating economic life, it is doubtful whether industries are more concentrated now than they were forty years ago. In the USA, indeed, the high point of monopoly had been reached in the opening years of the twentieth century. It was obvious even then that competition has not disappeared. Since then small companies have multiplied while big companies have grown. A few may compete as vigorously as many, and no longer do today's leaders seek to destroy all competition.

Monopoly is also weakened by the extent to which business has become international. It could have been argued at one time that the automobile market in the USA was shared between General Motors, Ford and Chrysler and that any tacit agreement between these three would have established an area of very imperfect competition. But the market has since been invaded by Volkswagen and Fiat, by British Leyland and Renault, by Toyota and Honda.

For purposes of export the market is world-wide, one country's sophistication of mass production being matched by another country's lower wage levels. Efforts have been made in the USA to prevent monopoly by legislation, but the real limits are set by foreign competitors. ICI occupies a stronger position in Britain than does any one chemical combine in the USA, but it has to face the competition of other giant concerns in Germany and Switzerland. There does not exist, nor has there ever been, a world monopoly in oil, steel, chemicals, copper, aluminium or rubber. Monopoly is also remote from the world of automobiles and tractors, electrical equipment and business machinery. It may have been possible to say at various times that a certain corporation like Ford or IBM had a decisive lead or a commanding position, but monopolies have been few and short lived. Where they have been established, moreover, by law or government regulation, as in a franchise given to a named airline on an internal route, they have seldom been outstandingly profitable. Real difficulties confront a small concern in attempting to invade the territory of an existing combine, but that is no proof that a monopoly exists. Where there are real monopolies they have been mostly created by left-wing governments in accordance with socialist theory. If big business is to be accused of establishing monopoly, the verdict must be 'not guilty'.

It is probably unfair to blame any single economist for giving currency to the monopoly myth. We cannot even attribute the mistake to Karl Marx. The fact is that the myth is almost as old as mankind. The complaint has always been that ruthless men have carved out vast estates for themselves, destroying villages and dispossessing thousands. The rise of the upstart is always noticed and deplored. If we studied only the literary sources we should wonder how any small enterprise ever managed to survive. A closer study of actual properties, whether agricultural, commercial or industrial, will reveal that the formation of large estates is largely balanced by the opposite tendency, the fragmentation of estates which were formerly as large. The difference lies in the publicity which surrounds the one process and the obscurity which hides the other. The spendthrift landowner avoids drawing attention to the piecemeal sale of his property, hoping to conceal, or at least postpone, his loss of consequence. The failing merchant has no reason to reveal the fact that a share of his business has been bought by someone else. The manufacturer keeps quiet about the transaction by which one of his factories is lost. Formerly

OVERLEAF Free trade propaganda from the days of the anti-protection debate.

CHEESE 6d lb

BACON 7½d lb

FREE TRADE SHOP

SUGAR 2d lb

SUGAR 2d lb

4D

BUTTER 1/- lb

TEA 1/6 PER lb

EGGS 20 for 1/-

JAM 10d PER 3lb

PICKLES 1/-

FREE TRADE

PUBLISHED BY THE LIBERAL PUBLICATI

PROTECTION SHOP
BACON 10d lb
4d
SUGAR 3½d lb
SUGAR 3½d lb
CHEESE 10d lb
RATES
PROTECTION
DESIGNED & PRINTED BY NATHANIEL LLOYD & Co LONDON
EPARTMENT. 42 PARLIAMENT STREET. S. W.

prosperous families sink back into obscurity without a sound, while all our attention is focused on the meteoric rise of the more fortunate. Companies are like families. Once their heyday is past no one will bother to chronicle the several transactions which mark their decline and fall. Our only surprise is in noting, occasionally, the continued existence of some company we had regarded as bankrupt. We had thought, we tell each other, that it had died some years ago.

Big business has come a long way since the early chaotic, experimental days of the nineteenth century. Industrial leaders are today more self-effacing and remote, although the world of high finance and stock-market manipulation continues to produce its Blooms and Cornfelds. The public has grown to live with big business, but this is partly because big business has learned to live with the public.

OPPOSITE *'Oh, if only you were here to help us.'* A cartoonist's view of the boardroom.

The 'C' from the Coca-Cola sign in Piccadilly Circus, London.

2 THE GIANTS EMERGE

The giant, international corporation is a feature of the modern world. In country after country the same names – most of them American – appear. Mobil, Coca-Cola, Nestlé, and a host of others are ubiquitous. And their influence is increasing. One estimate suggests that by 1988 there will be about three hundred international giants dominating the world's business.

Corporations are often akin to miniature states, while international concerns frequently conduct diplomatic negotiations with national governments as though they too were sovereign states. Corporations gain solidity by having an identity of their own. Many of them have an ancestry far longer than the majority of countries in the United Nations. Even in Europe the notorious firm of Krupp has survived the 1848 revolution, the rule of Bismarck, and all the dismal consequences of the First and Second World Wars. It continues to exist today without its founding family. The oldest corporation in the world is Stora Kopperberg in Sweden, which has a history stretching back to 1288. In that year a bishop bought a share in a copper mine. The original mine is still being worked by the company, which now has the largest paper mills and steelworks in Sweden.

What is the biggest industrial organization in the world today? On most counts the title must go to General Motors, that huge Detroit-based multinational, whose subsidiaries include Opel in Germany, Vauxhall in Britain, and Holden in Australia. Above all, General Motors leads the way if we take as our criterion either value of sales (as we usually do), or employment. The next biggest corporation is also American, Standard Oil of New Jersey ('Esso', as the first two initials are pronounced); and so is the third, the Ford Motor Corporation. Indeed, a catalogue of the world's largest concerns reads very much like a list of the USA's biggest enterprises: General Electric, IBM, Mobil, Chrysler, International Tel and Tel, Texaco and so on. A few European interlopers creep in. The Royal Dutch Shell group out-distances General Electric, while Unilever follows Chrysler. But in all, some fourteen of the top twenty companies in the

1902, fire at the Spindle-top field when Joseph S. Cullinan, the founder of the Texaco company, saved the day.

world are American based. The USA is indeed the home of big business.

Such a list gives a fair though not completely accurate picture of big business. Asset value, another commonly accepted criterion, yields the sort of results just given, but if we were interested in, say, employment, then Unilever, with its countless thousands of employees in West African plantations would come far higher up the list. Indeed, outside the USA the leading employers are Philips and Unilever, though they do not even begin to approach those of the great Royal Dutch Shell. However, we must remember that the USA is a country with more than two hundred million people, and concerns like Philips in the Netherlands, or Nestlé in Switzerland, have a far more powerful impact on their respective countries than General Motors has on the USA. Moreover, these firms are confined to the non-communist world. Russian industries are very big business indeed, Aeroflot being the world's leading airline. It is very clear, however, that in the capitalist world, big business is biggest in the USA. Moreover, a few basic products dominate the biggest concerns. Indeed, seven of the top twenty firms deal with one product, oil, and four are producers of motor vehicles. If we continued the list beyond the first twenty, we would find Boeing Aircraft, EI du Pont de Nemours (chemicals), Shell Oil (New York), ICI of Britain, British Steel and Goodyear Tyre and Rubber. Continuing the list still further, we find repeated and significant mention of Japan, with Hitachi, Toyota, Matsushita, Mitsubishi and Nissan.

We must not forget, also, that behind the giant organizations are the smaller firms who supply them with components. Shell, the Anglo-Dutch oil company, has no less than five hundred subsidiary and associated companies. Unilever has about the same number and ICI has over three hundred and fifty. It is true that these may be minnows in the wake of a whale but the minnows are at least alive. Of the Concorde Anglo-French supersonic jet-liner it can be said

Henri Nestlé, the Swiss founder of the giant Nestlé company. Nestlé began life as a chemist, but it was his development of the process of canning dried milk which led to the success of his company.

in the same way that hundreds of firms have played a part, many of them quite small and some employed in design rather than production. Apart from companies which are actually subsidiary to one of the giants, there are many others, regular suppliers, which come within a certain sphere of influence. It could be said of these that their independence is nominal but the fact remains that they continue to flourish and it would seem from the statistics, that they even become more numerous. Publicity is often given to the process by which smaller firms are absorbed into major groups. Far less attention is paid to the opposite process by which a division of a big group is made into a separate company. This happens, however, quite frequently, reminding us that the great combines are not, in fact, insatiable. Predictions have been made that the major industries will all be absorbed by the big companies. This could happen, no doubt, but we have very little reason to regard it as certain.

Turning again to the concerns of the giants, oil is obviously king, taking the place once held by steel, and the motor vehicle is central to our way of life. For the remainder of this chapter we will look more closely at the origins of some of these powerful industries and firms. Their stories are interesting in themselves, and they also remind us of the diversity of backgrounds from which the giants have emerged.

Oil, 'black gold' as it was once called, is synonymous with wealth, and with huge international companies.[1] Go to a remote Thailand village: there will be a friendly 'Gulf' sign to greet you. Journey to the romantic shores of Lake Victoria: 'BP', 'Shell', and the other oil giants will be vying with 'Coca-Cola' to attract you. Oil really is the biggest and the most international of all enterprises. The huge companies conduct their affairs across national boundaries. Any one company might operate in a hundred different countries. And despite the colossal scale of the oil sales outside the communist world, more than half are in the hands of the Big Seven, five of which are American, one British, and one jointly British and Dutch.

This huge industry is not very old. Oil springs and surface bubblings had been known, it is true, for centuries, and oil had many uses. In the Caucasus the tribes set fire to it and worshipped it; elsewhere it was used as a medicine, a lubricant, and a source of light. But only in 1859 was the first well drilled and the first major oilfield discovered. The discovery was due to the efforts of an eccentric enthusiast, 'Colonel' Edwin L. Drake. Known always as 'Colonel', although the only uniform he ever actually wore was that of a railroad conductor, Drake struck oil in the summer of 1859 in Titusville, Pennsylvania. The scene resembled the gold rushes in California a decade before, and very soon dozens of small wells were in operation with soaring output and, eventually, catastrophically falling prices. Some speculators made their fortunes; many lost everything. Poor Drake died virtually a pauper twenty-one years after his momentous discovery.

The chaos of early production methods, with hordes of small-scale operators, no huge companies to regulate output, and no firm with sufficient capital to operate on the most economical scale, set the scene for the rise of John D. Rockefeller, one of history's master-capitalists. Rockefeller was born in 1839. Like Carnegie, Ford and Morgan, he was strongly influenced by a deeply religious mother, and throughout his life never doubted that the many enemies he made in his business dealing were God's enemies also. At sixteen he started as a book keeper with a small firm of commission agents, but was soon in business on his own account, in partnership with a young English immigrant, Maurice Clark. Their firm prospered greatly during the Civil War in the early 1860s, dealing in a host of products, including Drake's new wonder, kerosene.

Cleveland, where Rockefeller lived, was a natural centre for oil refineries, being in excellent communication with the producing regions and with the major markets. Among several early refineries was one worked by Samuel Andrews, who came from the same Wiltshire village as Maurice Clark. In 1863 Rockefeller, Clark and Andrews formed their own refining company which by 1865 was the largest in Cleveland. The combination of Andrews' technical brilliance and Rockefeller's unflagging work and financial flair led to rapid growth. By 1870 Rockefeller was ready to incorporate the venture, and he became President of the Standard Oil Company.

Rockefeller's ambition was to concentrate oil refining, not only in Cleveland, but in New York, Pittsburgh, and throughout the USA. One huge concern could regulate output, and by virtue of its power, keep under control the demands of the rapacious railroad companies on which the refiners depended for transportation. So Rockefeller started buying up other refiners. Already by the end of 1871 Standard Oil was probably the biggest refinery in the USA. Starting with some ten per cent of the nation's total refining capacity at the beginning of the 1870s, by 1879 Rockefeller controlled about ninety per cent of this vastly increased capacity.

John D. Rockefeller,
creator of the notorious
Standard Oil Trust.
Bribery, corruption and
brutal business methods
enabled him to become
one of the richest men
in history and one of the
greatest philanthropists.

Rockefeller's business methods were brutal, and he fought competitors relentlessly. His monopoly position enabled him to dominate the railroads, obtaining huge concessions for Standard while his rivals paid exorbitant charges. Two huge struggles led to Standard absorbing the Empire Transportation Company's oil interests (refineries, pipelines and tank wagons) in 1877 and the Tidewater Pipe Company in 1883. Thus Rockefeller came to control an industrial empire which not only had an almost complete stranglehold on refining, but which also dominated the railroads and the pipelines.

At this time Rockefeller undertook a drastic reorganization of his monolithic company. In 1882 he created the Standard Oil Trust, the first of the USA's great and notorious trusts. The trust was established in Ohio, and controlled the operations of numerous subsidiaries throughout the country. This solved the problem of unifying management at a time when it was illegal for a company in one state to operate a subsidiary elsewhere. When, in 1892, Ohio State dissolved the trust (because so few of the trustees lived in Ohio), Rockefeller moved his headquarters to the more liberal New Jersey, and the Standard Oil Company (New Jersey) was formed.

Throughout this time Rockefeller, in building up the biggest industrial enterprise history had yet seen, had continued to ensure his monopoly with a ruthlessness which stood out even in the industrial jungle of the USA. He eliminated opponents by selective price-cutting. In 1892, for example, Standard sold kerosene in Denver for $7\frac{1}{2}$ cents a gallon in order to drive a rival out of business. Elsewhere the price was twenty-five cents. When retailers sold oil from Standard's competitors, he bankrupted them by driving prices down. Rockefeller paid fees to railroad clerks, so that he could receive information about who was taking supplies from whom. He also bribed the employees of his rivals to tell him their plans and what concessions they were receiving from the railroads.

No single firm could dominate an industry the way Standard did for long. Abroad, Standard's export position was eroded by competition from Russia during the 1880s, while at the end of the century powerful new rivals were emerging in the USA itself. The Texas oil industry started in 1901 when the famous Spindletop well sent a fountain of oil hundreds of feet in the air. New refineries sprang up, and names like 'Gulf' and 'Texaco' rose to prominence. After Texas came Oklahoma and Louisiana. Things could never be the same again. Moreover Standard was now attacked by the US Government as part of the 'trust-busting' activities of President Theodore Roosevelt. After years of legal battles, during which time Standard's competitors became even more powerful, the company was dissolved by the Supreme Court. Rockefeller, who had already given up executive responsibility in 1897, resigned the presidency, sold his shares (except one, which he kept for sentimental reasons) and watched his enterprise split into more than thirty regional companies. Many have prospered, and today Standard Oil of New Jersey is still the largest oil company in the world. Mobil (formerly Standard Oil of New York) is third, and three more are in the top ten.

Rockefeller was an enigma to his contemporaries, and remains so to historians. He typified the industrial ogre of muckraking literature. He was stern, withdrawn and ruthless. Yet outside his business he was kind, generous and deeply religious. All his life he gave away money, and when he died in 1937 (leading industrialists of the past seem to have lived a remarkable length of time) he had given away some $550 million and established the Rockefeller Foundation which has ranked his name with those of Carnegie and Ford among the great industrial philanthropists. Rockefeller never lost his own sense of righteousness, nor doubted that US industry needed discipline, coherence and order. When he said: 'mere money-making has never been my goal' it is just possible that he meant it.

During the early days Rockefeller's kerosene was used by humble peasants throughout the world as well as in the houses and thoroughfares of more civilized parts. The first serious competition came, oddly enough, from Russia. Oddly, for Russia was then an extremely backward country, only on the threshold of her industrial upsurge. Indeed, it is worth remembering here that with the notable exception of the USA, where oil was first discovered, most of the world's oil supplies are located in backward, scarcely habitable regions. This provides one very important explanation for that outstanding characteristic of the oil industry, its internationalism, for the poverty-stricken lands of Central America and the Middle East could hardly by themselves have built up a major capital-intensive enterprise like the oil industry.

Oil had long been known to exist in the Caucasian provinces of Russia, but not until 1873 was outside enterprise and capital forthcoming in sufficient amounts, from the legendary Nobel

Esso public relations announce their new 'attractively sited and designed' service station in Middlesex, England – an opinion which attenders of the church on the left of the picture would no doubt agree with.

Sir Marcus Samuel
(1798–1870), who chose
the famous Shell emblem
because of his earlier
business with sea-shells.
He was the first man to
send oil tankers through
the Suez Canal and
breach the Standard
Oil monopoly.

brothers of Sweden, to refine it. They started production in 1873, and their venture was soon joined by other wealthy fortune seekers, Russian and non-Russian. The powerful Rothschild family from Paris created another major company, the Black Sea Company, and Russian oil was soon competing with Standard all over the world. Indeed for a brief couple of years, in 1900 and 1901, Russia was actually the world's foremost producer. That was before crippling riots in the Caucasus and the 1905 Revolution throttled Russian production, and before the great Texan gushers had left their indelible mark on the world's oil trade.

Standard soon encountered other assailants. Among these was the remarkable Shell enterprise, whose symbol is familiar all over the world. Marcus Samuel (1835–1927) and his brother controlled the small trading company of M Samuel and Company, set up by their father in 1830. Their main commerce was with the Far East, and they dealt in a wide variety of products. Most of their trade was with Japan, a remote, little-known country, only recently opened to foreign trade. Searching for new products to sell, Samuel dealt with kerosene, and quickly saw the possibilities presented by the new illuminant. He chose his Shell emblem because exotic shells were among the products dealt in by the company. Soon he entered into agreement with Rothschild's Bankers' Company to provide him with oil for his historic enterprise: to send oil in bulk through the Suez Canal by tanker. Such a project startled the oil world, and most thought it impracticable and dangerous. But in 1892, Samuel's first tanker, the *Murex*, passed through the Suez Canal, discharging part of her cargo at Pulo Bukum, Singapore, and taking the rest to Bangkok. Having breached the Standard Far East monopoly, Samuel wanted to shorten the distance for his tankers by finding oil in South East Asia. Oil had been found in Burma, but Samuel's trial borings were in Dutch Borneo, where some more oil was found. The discovery was overshadowed, however, by one made in Sumatra by the Royal Dutch Company. Faced with this competition, Samuel turned to Texas and bought half the Texan supply for the next twenty-one years. With this he hoped to break Standard's monopoly in Britain. However, his financial backing was insufficient and the final result was that Shell amalgamated with Royal Dutch to form the predominantly Dutch company which now comes second in importance to Standard Oil of New Jersey. Although the first chairman was Sir Marcus Samuel (later Lord Bearsted) the victor in the battle, and

An artist's impression of a hand-dug oil well in Burma, *c.* 1900.

the controlling genius of the company was Henri Deterding. This Anglo-Dutch group developed oilfields in Sumatra and Borneo and gained a considerable share of the Far East market. Using Texas oil, it also invaded Britain and Europe. For further supplies, however, Deterding turned to Mexico and then to Venezuela, which had, as it turned out, the richest oilfield in the world. Venezuela's oil boom began shortly after the First World War, and the country soon became one of the world's leading producers.

British efforts to find oil did not begin and end with those of Shell. It was a British team which struck oil in Persia, between Baghdad and Teheran, a success which led to the formation of the Anglo-Persian Gulf Company, with its oil refinery at Abadan. By 1914 the oil was flowing and the British Government bought a controlling interest in the company which provided Britain with much of her oil supply in the First World War. This is the origin of BP which continues to rank among the major brand names of petroleum.

The Russian Revolution of 1917 closed the oilfield of Baku to international trade, reducing the world's supply drastically at a time when the mass production of motor vehicles was increasing the world's thirst for oil. More oil had to come from somewhere and the most

'Once more round the block O loved ones. We've got to use the damn stuff up somehow.' A cartoonist's view of the Arab sheiks at the time of Suez.

OPPOSITE In 1931 this was the latest word in petrol pumps.

hopeful source seemed to be Mesopotamia, now called Iraq, where the Turkish Petroleum Company (formed in 1912) already had exploration under way. Other companies were interested, however, and the eventual result was the agreement of 1927 which created the Iraq Petroleum Company. This was initiated as a joint undertaking by Shell, the Deutsche Bank, and Anglo-Persian – the sponsors of the Turkish Petroleum Company organized by G. S. Gulbenkian, who was allotted five per cent for his pains – together with the other major companies of the world. Oil was struck soon afterwards at Kirkuk in Iraq, making Gulbenkian's fortune, and supplies were plentiful again. IPC had been given, by international agreement, the right to exploit the oil resources of the Arabian Peninsula together with Iraq, Syria, Jordan and Turkey, but it showed no immediate interest in the possibilities of Bahrain and Kuwait. The result was that Standard Oil (California) took up the option in Bahrain, striking

oil there in 1932, and Gulf Oil took up the option in Kuwait, which turned out to be richer still. The Middle East pattern was complete, at least for the time being, when the Pacific Western Company, owned by J. Paul Getty, obtained a valuable lease in Saudi Arabia, and when a new and important oilfield was opened in Libya.

Subsequent events have proved the political instability of most Middle East countries, coupled with their tendency to break agreements. This trend has been exemplified by Libya, which took over the British Petroleum oilfield in 1971, and again by Iraq which nationalized the Iraq Petroleum Company's Kirkuk oilfield at much the same time. The record in Persia (Iran) is one of greater stability, especially since the present Shah overthrew the revolutionary Moussadek in 1953. This led to an agreement in 1954 which placed the Iranian oilfields, although nationalized, under the control of a consortium of eight leading companies for the next twenty-five years. The world pattern of oil supply has been further changed by the closing of the Suez Canal, the eventual result of its 'nationalization' (or theft) by Egypt and the Arab-Israeli wars of 1956 and 1973. These have emphasized the urgent need to find new oil supplies in Europe. Good results are expected from the North Sea and it seems probable that the Middle East sources will eventually lose their importance.

On land, oil is usually sent to its destination by rail or by pipeline. At sea it is usually carried in a specially made ship, the oil tanker. The first tanker was the Nobels' small *Zoroaster* of 1879, followed by other specialized ships for service on the Caspian Sea, whence the oil was distributed by iron barges on the great river Volga. Oceanic tankers, as we have seen, were introduced by Marcus Samuel in 1892. The *Murex* was four thousand tons and the other ships of the Shell fleet were little bigger. They grew in size, however, and some of them were as big as fourteen thousand tons by 1939. All the major oil companies had their own and they were among the finest merchantmen afloat, some with a speed of sixteen knots compared with the average of twelve. As an illustration of how vital the oil supply has become to the twentieth-century world, one could cite the perilous situation of Malta in 1942. Cut off from its normal supplies, the island was almost deprived of oil and it was only through a heroic effort that the tanker *Ohio*, mortally wounded, broke through the blockade and discharged her cargo of kerosene and fuel oil so that: 'the last gallon left her and simultaneously her keel settled gently on the bottom'. *Ohio* had saved Malta but perished in that final effort. Without oil the modern world comes to a standstill. Without oil the modern community is dead.

Steel too is a basic necessity of modern society. Like oil, steel became big business in the USA during the last quarter of the nineteenth century, and was also dominated for a long time by one man. These products, and the giant, wealthy enterprises they spawned, symbolized the sudden emergence of the USA as the world's leading industrial nation. Britain's days of supremacy were over. When in 1900, the huge United States Steel corporation was formed, it was the largest single industrial firm in the USA, and indeed in the world. Today, nearly three-quarters of a century later, it is still the largest steel business in existence.

To a remarkable extent this vast steel industry was the creation of one man, Andrew Carnegie.[2] This tough, small, effervescent

Scotsman returned to Pittsburgh from a European trip in 1872 convinced that he had seen an invention destined to reshape modern industry, the new steel-making process of Sir Henry Bessemer. The invention seemed to Carnegie to offer boundless opportunities. Already a millionaire and planning retirement, though not yet forty, Carnegie determined to build up a giant steel industry. For the USA had virtually no steel industry in 1872. Most of her steel rails were imported from Britain, and Britain, the home of the industrial revolution, seemed assured of a long ascendancy. Ten years later US steel production soared past that of Britain. Carnegie, and the age of US industrial dominance, had arrived.

If Carnegie remains something of an enigma, it is because it is difficult to understand how a man who could so generously give away over $350 million in his lifetime could drive such hard bargains with his competitors, or indeed with his partners. It is difficult to understand how a man so naïve in his judgements of world affairs could choose his henchmen so brilliantly, and sense the ebbs and flows of business cycles so instinctively. Certainly Carnegie's start in life was unpromising, and his story serves as a magnificent example of the self-made millionaire. He began penniless, and ended with the largest personal fortune in the world.

Andrew Carnegie came to America in 1848 at the age of thirteen. His father, William, was one of the countless handloom weavers made destitute by the rapidly spreading power looms in industrial Britain. With his wife Margaret, and two sons, Andrew and Thomas, William left his native Dunfermline in the 'year of glorious revolutions' and the Great Charter (he was himself a radical Chartist) and sought a new life across the Atlantic. They settled in Allegheny, across the river from Pittsburgh, and Andrew had at once to start work as a bobbin boy in a cotton mill. William struggled on desperately, and vainly, as a handloom weaver – the only craft he knew. He died, a failure, in 1855, at the age of fifty. His eldest son, however, went from strength to strength, and flourished in the competitive climate of the fast-growing United States. His first wage packet was $1.20 a week. By the age of fifteen he had become messenger boy for the newly established Pittsburgh telegraph, at $2.50 a week. Soon he merited a rise, and he wrote afterwards:

On Sunday morning I produced the two extra dollars and a quarter ... then Father's glance of loving pride and Mother's blazing eyes, soon wet

Andrew Carnegie, whose multi-million empire began at the age of fifteen when he earned $1.20 a week as a messenger boy, and who eventually became the richest man in the world. Carnegie's steel profits were founded on his overriding insistence on lowering costs and by this means he consistently managed to undercut his rivals.

The humble cottage in Dunfermline, Scotland, where Andrew Carnegie was born in 1835, the son of a poor handloom weaver.

with tears, told their feelings, it was their boy's triumph and proof positive that he was worthy of promotion. No subsequent success, or recognition of any kind, ever thrilled me as this did.

Andrew's precepts for business success were simple, but they worked. In the first place he scorned financiers and bankers: 'I sell steel, not securities,' he remarked. This scorn led him to oppose corporate enterprise for his plants, and he stuck to partnerships. This was certainly remarkable, for joint-stock enterprise is commonly supposed to be the key to modern industrial growth, and certainly a reason for the colossal industrial growth in the USA. Yet here was Carnegie, forming partnerships in each of his many businesses, ploughing back profits and relying on internal finance. He chose his partners uncommonly well, his thrusting young executives playing a significant part in the expansion of his empire. Some partners were brought in from the firms which he acquired. Such a man was Henry Clay Frick who owned vast coke plants which Carnegie needed to integrate with his own blast furnaces.

Frick was thirty-three when he merged his twelve thousand coke ovens with Carnegie's steel interests in 1882. At forty he was made president of Carnegie's enterprises and was clearly earmarked to be successor to Carnegie until the two men had an irreparable disagreement, and Frick's interests with Carnegie Steel were severed. But as time went by Carnegie increasingly picked out bright young men from among his employees, gave them the incentive of partnership, and then watched their force and diligence increase profits. The best-known example of these home-grown products was Charles Schwab. Taken on as a boy at a dollar a day, he rose to be an assistant manager in six months; within five years was a superintendent; by the age of thirty he was president of Carnegie Steel. Another Carnegie man was William Jones, a technical genius at a time when technique was at a premium. Jones is usually recognized as the man responsible for making the Bessemer Process successful in the USA. Having started as a two-dollars a day mechanic, Jones refused a partnership on the grounds that his men would then cease to trust him.

The castle which Carnegie bought in his native Scotland. Although he enjoyed personal extravagance, he once wrote an article entitled 'The Disgrace of Dying Rich', and by the time of his death in 1919, had given away over $350 million.

He told his employer: 'Just give me a hell of a salary if you think I'm worth it.' So Carnegie promptly paid him the same salary as that of the President of the United States.

A further principle followed by Carnegie was to use depressions as a time to invest. For most people, to commence a huge new business venture at the beginning of a widespread trade slump, such as happened in 1873, would be improbable. For Carnegie, depressions were rather a time of opportunity, when costs were lowest. His optimism led him never to doubt that revival would come, and, when it did, the Carnegie plants would be the best equipped and most modern in the country, able to undercut their competitors in a booming market. And, of course, the nature of a cycle is that an upturn does come. In the depressions of 1873, 1883 and 1893 Carnegie poured forth huge outlays and bought out competitors at rock-bottom prices. In times of prosperity his profits soared. In 1896 they stood at six million dollars and in 1900 had reached forty million. Carnegie's business philosophy was well suited to the grasping competitive age in which he lived. He had no interest in prices, only costs. The market set the price, and it was the job of Carnegie's plant managers to lower costs to the utmost so that at any ruling market price Carnegie would be in a position to undersell all other competitors.

Carnegie was a restless man, and often considered retirement, but did not do this until 1900, aged sixty-five. Retirement was no simple matter, with such a huge company, for no single individual could buy him out. Eventually he permitted the great banker John Pierpont Morgan to set up the United States Steel Corporation – a giant trust. The price was four hundred million dollars plus a ninety-two million-dollar bonus of common stock which Carnegie insisted be confined to his partners – he was content with his own share of over $250 million.

Carnegie was an enigmatic, extraordinarily complex character. He enjoyed his wealth and prestige and yet he was always conscious of the burden of social responsibility it entailed. Mark Twain wrote: 'That foxy, white-whiskered, cunning little face, happy, blessed, lit up with a sacred fire, and squeaking, without words, "Am I in Heaven or is it only a dream?"' Carnegie himself wrote: 'wealthy men should set a pattern of simplicity', yet he had a castle in Scotland and a mansion on Fifth Avenue. He had tartan wallpaper in New York and had bagpipes as well as yachts and carriages. He enjoyed

Inside the steelworks: bombs being manufactured in 1941. The molten metal was ladled in, and half an hour later the metal was tipped out, like the yoke of an egg.

entertaining and meeting the great – Matthew Arnold, Gladstone, Mark Twain, Herbert Spencer, Lloyd George, Paderewski and Tchaikovsky – and he boasted about his acquaintances. Mark Twain once wrote: 'I don't believe I can stand the King Edward story again.' Carnegie was very attached to Scotland and the scenes of his youth. He was also devoted to his mother and never minded her frequent visits to his office, or even her presence at managers' meetings. Indeed, he never married until after his mother's death, in 1886, when he was fifty-one. In 1889 Carnegie wrote an article: 'The Disgrace of Dying Rich', and in it he proposed that the wealthy should give away money. In 1900 the same theme was repeated in his book, *The Gospel of Wealth*. After his retirement, he spent fifteen years working hard to give away money. Increasingly he became interested in social problems, and above all in projects for world peace. He set up foundations, trusts, and endowed numerous good causes. He rewarded US military heroes, and gave pensions to all Civil War telegraphers who were not provided for out of public funds. He built libraries, museums, and endowed schools and universities. In all he distributed more than $350 million. It was the outbreak of the First World War which shattered his faith, an event which he had believed impossible. In 1913 the Peace Palace at the Hague had been built with money provided by Carnegie. Ironically, the gala celebration to mark its opening was planned for the fateful month of August 1914. Carnegie was an invalid from 1915, living until 1919 and dying at the age of eighty-three. The world he knew and understood had passed away.

It is perhaps significant that the nineteenth century ended with steel as the central focus of big business enterprise. Steel, basic to so many goods, above all to the railways, symbolized the industrial revolution in the nineteenth century. Here was a huge capital goods industry, pioneering a new technology, and promising a new age of economic growth. In the twentieth century, the age, as Professor Rostow calls it, of 'high mass consumption', the car has taken pride of place. Within a generation it ceased to be a luxury and became a new way of life. By the close of the First World War a car-producing firm had become the largest company in the world. Most of the great – and small – firms in the motor business commemorate their founders, men such as Citroën, Ford, Chrysler, Morris, Renault and Daimler. The exception is General Motors. This, the world's largest corporation, had its origins in 1908, when William C. Durant of the Buick Company made one concern out of seventeen, including Cadillac and Oldsmobile. The year 1908, which saw the birth of Ford's 'Model T' and the formation of General Motors, is a significant date in the history of the motor industry. Durant's company concentrated on the medium and upper range of products (the du Ponts brought their Chevrolet business into General Motors in 1917), but in the cheap bracket Ford swept all before him. By 1910 nearly half the cars produced in the USA were Model T's: soon the share was more than half. As in so many fields, fortune favoured the biggest. Gradually

On the sign in image:
THE PARK COMMISSIONERS HEREBY FORBID ANY ONE FROM DEPOSITING ANY FILTH, OR RUBBISH ON THIS BEACH, UNDER PENALTY OF LAW. A WRITTEN APPLICATION WILL BE REQUIRED BY THE PARK COMMISSIONERS TO ENABLE ANY PERSONS TO ERECT, OR MAINTAIN ANY BATH HOUSE, OR OTHER STRUCTURE ON THIS BEACH.

One of the fifteen-and-a-half-million Model T Cars, inspired and manufactured by Henry Ford. This car is a symbol of the revolution it wrought in the affairs of men. The Five Dollar Day, the age of mass production and of cars for the people were very much the result of the Model T, which, at its peak, rolled off the production line at the rate of one every fifteen seconds.

production was concentrated among fewer and fewer concerns. Even in 1912 half the cars were made by seven companies; in 1923 ninety per cent came from ten, and from 1925, when the brilliant Walter Chrysler formed his competitor to Ford and General Motors, the three companies never produced between them less than eighty per cent of the entire American output.

The huge success of General Motors was achieved as a result of the organizing genius of Alfred Sloan. In 1921 General Motors had twelve per cent of the US car market, but Sloan's drastic reorganization, involving the creation of five divisions, each to concentrate on a single price market, led to a rapid decrease in Ford's colossal lead. Cadillac, Oldsmobile, Buick, Oakland (later called Pontiac) and the new Chevrolet division all prospered under the new regime. By 1926 the value of General Motors' output was already greater than that of Ford's and the company soon achieved about sixty per cent of total American production, a proportion it has more or less retained.

But the pioneer of the giant motor company was undoubtedly

Henry Ford. In many ways Ford ushered in a new age, for his great plant at Dearborn on the river Rouge in Detroit was the earliest to use on a massive scale the powerful potential of the mass-production conveyor belt. In another way, Ford ended an era. When he died in 1947 he was the last of the great original founders of modern big business. Ford built his great manufacturing enterprise from a tiny workshop to a global giant. His achievement was of the same order as Carnegie, Rockefeller or Lever. But the very scale of present-day operations and the resources of capital they must control makes another such saga all but impossible.

Until the end of the Second World War, when senility and growing disillusionment finally induced Henry Ford to surrender control of his enterprise to his grandson, that great, hated, loved and ridiculed industrialist had personally ruled and dominated the Ford Motor Company for more than forty years. From its humble origins in 1903 the Ford Company had grown by the end of the First World War to be easily the largest motor company in the world. Ford's methods started a technological revolution, and his cars wrought a social revolution unparalleled in modern times. If ever an individual fashioned an industrial business, it was Henry Ford, and the history of the Ford Motor Company lies in the personality of its founder. How ironic that Ford's most famous saying was that 'history is bunk'!

Henry was born in 1863, in the middle of the American Civil War, on a farm in Michigan, near Dearborn. His father had emigrated from Ireland in 1847, at the time of the great famine, although he was in fact, English. Henry's upbringing was strict, and like Andrew Carnegie, he was strongly influenced by a deeply religious, evangelical mother. Hard work, for Henry, was a virtue. From an early age he showed a precocious aptitude for mechanics, and in old age he liked to pride himself that he could fashion each part of his cars by hand. This flair was to prove significant. Like Carnegie, Ford always distrusted financiers and speculators. Ironically, the possessor of the largest industrial fortune of his time railed against 'capitalists', preferring to think of himself as a worker. This itself was ironic, for Henry Ford came eventually to create more bitterness and hatred among his own employees than possibly any other employer in history. Unlike Carnegie, however, Ford's vision was confined to his factory. This was his strength and his weakness. Carnegie was a master salesman, Ford a master craftsman. Production and ever more production was the goal Ford set himself.

The public knows two Henry Fords. There is the kindly, benign Ford, a man of rough manners, down-to-earth humour and sound common-sense: an ordinary man made extraordinary by hard work and perseverance and his own mechanical and organizational genius. He was eccentric, of course – he detested cigarettes and allowed no one to smoke in his factories. He pronounced on public issues with the confidence of ignorance. He even, it is rumoured, set his sights on the Presidency of the United States, although he was in fact practically illiterate. He once described the word 'commenced' as a technical term, and claimed he seldom read books since 'they mess up my mind'. His idealism, at its most ridiculous, led him to sail for Europe in 1915 on a 'peace ship' that was to end the war. In business his cars brought untold benefits to untold numbers. His starting of the 'Five Dollar Day' in 1914 made him a great benefactor of the working-classes, while the establishment of the Ford Foundation in 1936 made him rank among the world's greatest philanthropists.

But there was the other Ford: the man who sacrificed partners, colleagues, workers, even family, to his god of mass production. There is a German word *Fordismus* which conjures up the epitome of maximum industrial productivity, where everything yields place to the tyranny of economic efficiency. The Five Dollar Day and the conveyor belt meant more money for the workers. It also meant insecurity, for skilled labour could be dispensed with, and the lure of high wages meant an assured pool of willing labour ready to step into the shoes of any dissatisfied or incompetent worker. Indeed, on the very day that the Five Dollar wage was announced, violence flared at the Dearborn factory as men clamoured for work. Ford was also a bigot, and a vigorous anti-Semite, who allowed his personal prejudices to govern his actions and his dealings with men.

How can we account for these contradictions? It is partly a question of time, for until the middle of the 1920s Henry Ford was a national folk hero, whose enterprise symbolized the American dream of earthly rewards for the ordinary self-made man. But as Ford grew older, his natural authoritarian views were fostered and made dangerous by his wealth. His words were power, and the yes-men around him did as their master wanted. Also, our views of Ford are conditioned by the people who write about him. Early biographies and his ghosted *My Life and Work* have the stamp of paranoid and sanctimonious self-justification. Recollections of the great depression have a totally different story to tell.

Henry's early mechanical flair induced him to leave his father's farm and, as a raw sixteen-year-old, seek employment as a mechanic in Detroit. He soon became acquainted with the new internal combustion engine, although he did not at first grasp its possibilities. Later, when working with the Edison Electric Company, he became fascinated with the new contrivance and set about building his own car in a workshop at the back of his house. He was no inventor, but he speedily learnt from others, and on 4 June 1896 a triumphant Henry Ford drove his first car round the streets in the early hours of the morning.

Ford was determined to produce and sell cars and gradually found enough backers to establish the Detroit Automobile Company in August 1899. Ford was then thirty-six. A new age was dawning.

But dawn was uncommonly long in breaking. The new company failed in little more than a year, and Ford decided to take up motor racing. In 1901 his new car broke the US speed record and, with this success behind him, he formed the Henry Ford Motor Company. But his interest in racing led him to part company with his brilliant engineer Henry Leland (who developed the Cadillac and the Lincoln),

Henry Ford's first car, the Quadricycle, which he built in 1869.

and he had to find new backing. As a result the present Ford Motor Company was incorporated in June 1903 with twelve shareholders and a paid-up capital for as long as Henry lived, for he issued no more stock. Almost at once he bought out a number of his fellow shareholders, and by 1906 had acquired a controlling interest. The Ford Motor Company was henceforth virtually the private property of one man.

Ford's wealth and success were based on one remarkable motor car, the Model T. The earliest automobiles were luxuries; expensive playthings for the rich. Henry Ford, however, turned to a different market – the vast middle layer of US society. A small, light vehicle was needed, and the Model T, introduced in 1908, proved the answer. Almost at once the new car caught the imagination of the American public. So successful was it, that in 1909 Ford was confident enough to make a momentous decision: one model only would be produced by his company, and the car would be one colour only. 'A customer can have a car painted any colour he wants so long as it is black,' he announced.

The Model T reached a popularity no car, even the Volkswagen 'Beetle', has ever equalled. At a time when poor roads made even a short journey an adventure, the 'Tin Lizzie' would go anywhere, on mud, snow, or desert. In 1911, a Model T was driven to the top of Ben Nevis. The following year one penetrated down into the Grand Canyon, and out again. Sales leapt. In the first full year over ten thousand were sold, an astonishing number. In 1913–14 output was a quarter of a million; in 1920–1 all but one million. By 1925 the Ford works were turning out ten thousand a day, and by 1926 some fifteen million Model T's had been produced. Henry Ford, the king of the motor industry, was a living legend, with world-wide fame.

Ford's miracle rested on standardization. His car was mechanically brilliant, and he organized production on the most modern lines. Like Carnegie, he was no inventor but when he was convinced a new idea was a winner he was prepared to back it with all his energy and drive. Ford's plants were not the first to use the moving conveyor-belt system of production, but they were the first to use it, once trials had proved successful by 1913, on such a massive and spectacular scale. The huge works at Dearborn, covering well over a square mile, were a temple to mass production. Raw iron came in one day; two days later it would emerge as a Model T. All processes were simplified as far as possible, and more than eighty separate operations were

involved in the manufacture of the engine alone. At its peak the plant was turning out a Model T every fifteen seconds, and by the mid-1920s Ford's works, supplying well over half the US market, could produce more cars in three months than the whole of Europe could in a year.

The great days did not, and perhaps could not, last long. Sales started to slip as powerful competitors like General Motors and Chrysler began to erode the phenomenal lead Ford had built up. Ford's adherence to a single, very basic car became a liability, as the American public began to look for something more stylish and less obviously mass-produced. Moreover, the very reliability of the Model T's posed formidable competition, as millions of second-hand Model T's came on the market. In May 1927, with sales slipping alarmingly, Henry Ford, now an old man of sixty-four, made another momentous decision. The Model T would be scrapped and the whole plant closed

Henry Ford (*left*) relaxing with Thomas A. Edison (*centre*) and US President Warren (*right*) on a camping trip in 1921.

MEN WANTED

for nearly a year, while experiments and machinery for a new car, the 'Model A', were undertaken. For a time the new car was very successful, but Ford's pre-eminence had gone for ever. When depression struck in 1929, sales of the Model A slumped quickly, and in 1933 Ford sold fewer cars than either General Motors or Chrysler. General Motors now assumed a lead among US, and world, producers which it has never relinquished.

The personality of Henry Ford continued to dominate the Ford company as the old man stumbled towards senility. He became increasingly suspicious of his subordinates, and allowed his only son Edsel (who had been nominal president of the company since 1918) little independence. Ford's weaknesses lay in the organization of his company, if 'organization' it can be called. He distrusted 'experts' and he avoided as far as possible specialized executive positions. In theory, any job at Dearborn was open to anyone, yet no job was safe, and many of Ford's leading executives were sacked. William Knudsen, who eventually became president of General Motors, left in 1921, during Ford's highly characteristic reaction to a catastrophic slump. This was to purge the organization (the office staff was cut by half), cut costs in every way, produce more at lower prices, and force thousands of cars upon the desperate dealers. Charles Serenson, for forty years a close associate of Henry Ford, was ultimately dismissed.

Ford had no time for organized labour, and for years set his face against the unions. Labour relations were in the hands of the notorious Ford Service Department, under a brutal character called Harry Bennett. Ford, in his declining years, came to rely heavily on this man, a former professional boxer, who brought a Darwinian belief in the survival of the fittest to his dealings with Ford employees. He always carried a gun and kept a target range in his office. Henry Ford, once the workers' champion with his Five Dollar Day, the man who considered himself an ordinary workman and hated the capitalists, became himself a byword for exploitation. Not unnaturally, therefore, among the scores of protest and hunger marches which occurred in the USA in the midst of the great depression, was one by Detroit's unemployed, aimed at the Dearborn plant. A procession of several hundred took place in the spring of 1932, and when Bennett arrived at the scene and stepped from his car, someone hurled a brick at his head. Immediately gunfire started, some from the Dearborn police, some from Ford's own company police (Ford actually had more police on his payroll than the whole of Detroit City). Four of the marchers were killed, and twenty were wounded. The tragedy confirmed Ford's hostility to unions, and confirmed his own evil reputation among workers. More years of violence followed, with Ford refusing to treat with the unions. Not until 1941 was his stand finally broken, and when his workers voted to unionize, Henry was amazed and shattered.

When Edsel Ford died in 1943, Henry became company president once more. Senility now added to the dangers of his personality. Not until 1945, at the age of eighty-two, did he finally yield power, and it was left to his grandson Henry Ford II to rebuild the shattered remains of the most famous automobile company in the world. Young Henry, not yet thirty, was suddenly thrust into one of the most difficult reconstruction tasks in industrial history. How he managed to re-create not only the profitability and standing of the Ford Motor Company, but also its image, is one of the miracles of modern industry. Today he is still at the helm. Certainly the shadow of old Henry was quickly lifted. The new leader almost at once, and to universal astonishment, sacked more than one thousand of the managerial staff. One of the first to go was Harry Bennett, who was a vice-president and had eyes on the top job. It is said that Henry went in person to Bennett's office and helped throw the furniture into the street. Old Henry lingered on, senile and miserable, until 7 April

'*As my father would have said. . . .*' A cartoonist's view of the family business.

1947. Henry Ford had become by then a part of the history he despised.

During Ford's lifetime the motor industry became more and more concentrated, and since his death, it has become even more so. The world's three major firms are all American, and they have a greater volume of sales than all the other companies put together. They all operate on a global scale, with subsidiaries in many parts of the world. Motor companies, indeed, were among the earliest of the huge multinationals, for Ford and Sloan were quick to see that proximity of markets, local assembly work, and manufacture inside a tariff wall, could prove very profitable. As early as 1919, General Motors tried to buy out the French Citroen works, and was similarly unsuccessful with an attempt to acquire both Austin and Morris in Britain. But in 1925 they were able to take over the small British Vauxhall company, and in 1929 acquired Adam Opel in Germany. The global spread of the American giants was well under way. Even the Holden, 'Australia's own car', as the advertisements say, is a General Motors product. American firms dominate the world motor industry, but within every country where it exists, either as a national concern or a multinational enterprise, the industry is highly concentrated. In Italy, for example, Fiat is overwhelmingly powerful, controlling three-quarters of the domestic market, while in France a few companies, Renault (which is in fact nationalized), Peugeot and Citroen dominate the industry. The huge British market is largely in the hands of four firms, British Leyland, Ford, Chrysler and Vauxhall, while in Germany, Ford, Opel and Volkswagen share most of the market between them.

As we have seen, automobile firms have grown partly by internal growth, as with Ford, and partly by acquisition and merger as with General Motors. British Leyland was the product of an amalgamation in 1968 between the near-bankrupt British Motor Corporation with the highly successful Leyland Motor Corporation to form one of Britain's largest industrial enterprises. The British Motor Corporation itself emerged from an amalgamation in 1951 between the two major British companies, Morris and Austin. The Austin Motor Company, established in 1906, preceded Morris by four years, while Lanchester had produced the first all-British motor car as early as 1895. But it was the Morris firm which rapidly gained ascendancy among Britain's manufacturers, and which came as near as any British concern to rivalling the American giants.

William Richard Morris, or 'W.R.M.' as he was always known, created the modern motor industry in Britain. From a modest beginning in 1910, he built up his vast organization. By the eve of the Second World War, Morris Motors was employing about one in four of all workers in Britain's motor industry. William Morris had none of the advantages of family wealth and connections, nor of a secondary education. He was born to poor parents in Worcester in

'We're bound to have teething troubles at first.' One view of the merger between BMC (who made Jaguars) and Leyland (who made heavy lorries).

1877, and went to a village school in the Oxfordshire hamlet of Cowley. He wanted to be a surgeon, but instead had to leave school early and went to work in a local bicycle shop. Morris combined mechanical flair with the ability to work long and hard, to exacting standards. Soon he was able to start a cycle repair shop of his own in Cowley High Street. At the same time he took up the newly popular sport of cycle racing, and won seven championships. By the time he

left his teens motor cars had begun to make their appearance on English roads. A host of small firms made specialized and expensive machines for the recreation of the wealthy. In the USA Henry Ford, as we have seen, was becoming aware of the prospect of a mass market for cars. Morris had a similar vision, and was excited by the prospects opened up by the new invention. He began to design a machine of his own and in 1910, at the age of thirty-three, completed the design of a car which he proposed to call the Morris Oxford. With little capital himself, he induced the Earl of Macclesfield to lend him an amount variously rumoured as between two thousand and thirty thousand pounds. He rented what was formerly a grammar school on the Cowley Road and erected a small works behind it. Armed only with blueprints, he sold four hundred cars at £165 each.

The Morris Oxford was an instant success, and was soon a familiar sight on Britain's roads. Checked by the First World War, Morris afterwards continued where he had left off. In 1920 he sold nearly two thousand cars at four hundred pounds each, and the following year, boldly slashing his price to £225 at the height of a crippling depression, managed to sell more than three thousand. The motor car was Britain's fastest growing industry, Morris its leading concern. In 1926 General Motors offered Morris eleven million pounds for his firm, an offer which was declined. Instead, Morris decided to incorporate his enterprise as Morris Motors Ltd, capitalized with three million one-pound shares and eight million five-shilling shares of common stock.

Morris was one of the earliest of Britain's big business leaders to

Morris cars near the Cowley works in Oxford. William Morris, another rags-to-riches big business man became, as Lord Nuffield, a donor of vast sums to charity.

be publicly honoured. In 1929 he received a baronetcy, and five years later was created Baron Nuffield of Nuffield. In 1938 he was made a Viscount. Yet he remained a simple man with simple tastes. Reminiscent of Ford, his constant boast was that he could design, make and sell any part of the vast range of vehicles he controlled. His mode of living was spartan, his capacity for work undiminished. His office remained the worm-eaten old headmaster's room in the grammar school on Cowley Road. He did not delegate power easily, another quality he shared with Ford, and, like Ford, he left a far from efficient organization when he departed. Preferring his own methods, Morris fell out with his deputy, L.P.Lord, just before the war, and Lord left to become managing director of Austin Motors. Again like Fords, Morris Motors was built up largely through the ploughing back of profits. Providing no more than a thousand pounds of his own money to start with, and repaying the Earl of Macclesfield as soon as he was able, Morris created a firm of which the cumulative profits had reached about thirty million pounds by the time of the Second World War.

Lord Nuffield soon joined the big industrial philanthropists. He set up the Nuffield Foundation, with nearly five million shares in his company, to promote scientific and medical research and to improve public health. At the same time he gave away over six million pounds in cash, much of it to Oxford University, where a new medical school was founded and Nuffield College was established. In recognition of his services the University made him a Doctor of Civil Laws, and he was so moved at the ceremony that he rose, interrupted the proceedings, and announced that he was contributing a further nine hundred thousand pounds.

Morris, Austin, Fiat, Renault, Ford, and most of the other great motor companies of today, outside Japan, can trace their histories back almost to the dawn of the automobile age. A notable exception is Volkswagen, Germany's major industrial concern, one of Europe's largest companies and, indeed, one of the world's top car-producing firms. *Volkswagenwerk* is a remarkable company, the post-war success of which is unique in the annals of big business. Volkswagen cars are sold in nearly every country in the world, and the famous 'Beetle' is a shape familiar in every country of western Europe and throughout Asia, America, Australasia and Africa. Most Volkswagen cars are produced in the giant Wolfsburg plant, where the firm is controlled by an all-German board. For many years the vast and

symmetrical factory at Wolfsburg has been a showplace of German industry. Situated in bleak country only a few miles from the borders of East Germany, Wolfsburg is wholly a company town, made by Volkswagen for Volkswagen.

The Volkswagen story began before the war when Hitler commissioned the great car designer, Ferdinand Porsche, to design a 'people's car'. Hitler himself laid the foundation stone at Wolfsburg in 1938, dedicating the promised car to the 'strength-through-joy' movement. But no Beetle was produced, for the plant was commandeered almost at once for wartime production. After the war the plant was in the hands of the British occupation army. One officer, Major Hirst, became interested in the quaint pieces of Volkswagen cars in the factory, and is supposed to have said, 'Might even build a few cars.' For a time, a proposal to transfer the plant to Britain in part payment of war reparations was mooted, but the British manufacturers saw little prospect of the ugly, noisy car being a commercial success. At one stage the plant was offered to the Americans, but they too saw no future for the strange machine. By 1947 the Allies were preparing to hand back factories to the Germans, and the British military authorities invited a forty-eight-year-old engineer, Heinz Nordhoff, to take over the Volkswagen works. Nordhoff himself wanted to return to the Opel company (controlled by America's General Motors) where he had worked during the war. But the Americans refused to accept anyone who had managed wartime industries.

Nordhoff, as it happened, was one of the great managers in the

Two other great names in car history – the Rootes brothers. Sir William (*left*) was the chairman, while Sir Reginald (*right*) his younger brother, doing the listening and smiling during a trans-atlantic telephone call, was the deputy chairman. The Rootes firm was eventually absorbed by Chrysler.

The incredible Volks-
wagen Beetle tells its own
story. By 1974 it had sold
nearly eighty million
models throughout the
world.

history of big business. He banked heavily on a single model, the Beetle, and despite numerous changes in detail the overall concept and appearance of the car remained unaltered, just as Porsche had envisaged. Nordhoff's hopes were more than fulfilled. Soon the Volkswagen dominated the German market; then it spread to Europe. In 1953 the Beetle invasion of Britain commenced, and by the end of the decade they were penetrating the USA. In 1967, indeed, more Volkswagens were sold in America than in Germany.

Volkswagen had always taken great care with its advertising campaigns, and these, together of course with the obvious virtues of the car, have helped make the Beetle the world's most exported car. The primitive Volkswagen is a rather humorous car, and this is reflected in many of the advertisements. An American advertisement, for example, showed a South American tycoon who was asked if his Volkswagen had air-conditioning: 'No, but I've got others in the deep freeze', came the reply. And in Germany, a slogan was plugged which read: 'Volkswagen, your second car, even if you haven't got a first'.

Nordhoff presided over the growing company with what he called 'the loneliness of unshared responsibility'. Until 1961 the company was state-owned, but in that year the government decided on de-nationalization although it still maintained a substantial holding. Nordhoff's position strengthened as the fortunes of the company grew.

But the great strength of the firm, its single model, was also its problem – an echo of the Model T once more. Certainly there were other cars produced by Volkswagen: buses, sports cars, vans, and variants of the Beetle, but the empire was founded on the Beetle, and this remains its mainstay. Since the latter half of the 1960s the Wolfsburg firm has been increasingly preoccupied with finding a successor for it. Nordhoff retired during 1967 and it remains to be seen whether the new leadership can revitalize the firm as Ford managed to do.

Nobody who visits Turin would be surprised to learn that the Fiat Motor Company is the largest of Italy's private corporations. The most spectacular of all the Italian private commercial empires, it remains firmly in the hands of the Agnelli family. The company dominates Turin, providing work for a hundred thousand people, making cars, lorries, railway engines, aeroplane engines, and steel. Its private health service looks after nearly a third of the inhabitants of Turin. It owns a whole suburb of tall flats, two seaside resorts (one of which has a sixteen-storey skyscraper), a hospital and an alpine camp. It owns the Turin daily newspaper, which is one of the best in Italy, *La Stampa*, and also owns Turin's largest insurance company. The firm runs an apprentices' school for a thousand boys, nearly all of whom are absorbed into the Fiat company. The firm finances engineering professors at Turin University. The bars and restaurants of Turin swarm with Fiat employees.

For more than seventy years Fiat has been an important part of Italy's economy. It was founded by a group of Turin businessmen under the name Fabbrica Italiana Automobili Torino, soon to be shortened to its initials. The first chairman was Giovanni Agnelli, a thirty-three-year-old cavalry officer who became one of the giants of modern enterprise. Brilliant, autocratic, and ruthless, Agnelli dominated Fiat for forty-five years, creating a huge industrial empire and amassing a gigantic personal fortune. When Agnelli died at the end of the last war, ownership passed to his eleven grandchildren. But the real control lay in the hands of Professor Vittorio Valletta, who for twenty years guided Fiat through a colossal period of expansion. Fiat became by far the biggest company in Italy, and in 1967 surged ahead of Volkswagen to become Europe's largest producer of cars.

One of the last of Valletta's achievements was the most sensational, and may possibly have consequences reaching far beyond industrial affairs. In 1966, after long negotiations, Valletta concluded a deal with the Russians. Fiat would collaborate in the construction of a huge plant on the river Volga designed to turn out six hundred thousand cars a year, three times Russia's current production, and over half Fiat's. The car was to be a modified version of Fiat's 124. Work began at once, and the new factory-town is steadily growing. To the fury of the Italian Prime Minister the Russians have insisted that the new town be called Togliattigrad, after the dead Italian communist leader.

When Valletta retired in 1966 the Agnelli family once more obtained control and Giovanni Agnelli took over as chairman. The eldest of the grandsons, he had been deputy chairman of Fiat, yet there was widespread astonishment at his succession. He is something of a legend in Italy, with an image not unlike that of Canada's Trudeau. After the war he was one of the dashing, sophisticated international set. His personal charm, good looks, great wealth, obvious love of power, and the luxurious trappings of yachts and a private helicopter, make him a figure constantly in the public eye. There is a continual stream of gossip and speculation about his wealth, power, women and secret political influence. He has a great admiration for the USA, and pays frequent visits there.

Under Valletta, Fiat had been tremendously successful. But its management structure was rigid: many of its key men were national rather than international in outlook. So Agnelli set about streamlining the company. He brought in a retiring age of sixty-five, sent young managers to the USA for training, and brought in banking and accounting experts from outside. At the same time he developed the international operations of the Fiat enterprise.

New developments may push Fiat even further into multinational enterprise. In May 1967 Agnelli suddenly heard that the nationalized Alfa Romeo planned to construct a plant near Naples to employ fifteen thousand workers and make three hundred thousand cars a year. The new model, the 'Alfa-Sud', is a popular, relatively low-priced car, and therefore directly competitive with some of Fiat's models. It had been tacitly understood that no rival would compete with Fiat in the popular car range, and Fiat's monopoly, producing some four-fifths of Italy's car output, would remain unchallenged. But political factors have played their part. The highly centralized Fiat works symbolize the prosperity and economic strength of Northern Italy, while the South has languished. And no amount of pressure and protest from Fiat has been able to dissuade the government from sanctioning a measure they believed would help bring prosperity to the South and prove politically popular.

Before we leave the motor industry, we will glance at one more firm, Japan's Toyota company. Japan, more than any other country, seems likely in the not too distant future to challenge the pre-eminence of US big business, and Toyota typifies the strength of the challenge. In terms of output Toyota is now the world's leading car producer outside the USA. In 1971 Toyota made 1.4 million cars, and Nissan-Datsun 1.1 million. By contrast, British Leyland produced in 1971 around 850,000 cars.

Toyota has grown from the genius of one of Japan's great inventors, Sakichi Toyoda. Toyoda designed what, forty years ago, were the most advanced automatic textile looms in the world. His company, called the Toyoda Automatic Loom Works, received a hundred thousand pounds in 1929 from a Lancashire company for the rights to produce the Toyoda looms in England, and with the money Toyoda

set about developing a car division of his company. After considerable investigation, Toyoda decided that the prospects for domestic production of small cars were good, and he put his son, Kiichiro, in charge of the new venture. By 1935 the first prototypes were ready. Kiichiro sent one of his engineers to the USA to study the techniques of mass production used there, so that the latest methods of assembly-line manufacture could be adopted. The engineer, on reaching Detroit, decided to go to the Packard works because this company offered convenient guided tours of the plant. For days the Toyoda man, unsuspected, mingled quietly with the tourists. Each evening in his hotel room he wrote up his notes and made sketches. Then he returned to Japan with his information, on which the first Toyoda assembly plant was based.

By 1937 the car division was large enough to be reorganized as a separate company, and at this stage the name was changed to Toyota. In Japanese, the word 'Toyoda' requires ten strokes of the pen, Toyota only eight. It is tempting to believe that this was an early example of raising productivity, although the reason given is that the number eight was considered more auspicious for the Toyoda family. Soon war engulfed Japan, and with it, of course, the nascent Toyota Motor Company. After the war the Japanese economy remained for long at a very low ebb, and in 1949 the tight money policy of the US occupation authorities pushed the firm to the brink of bankruptcy. Toyota was chronically short of cash, while the credit squeeze led many Toyota owners, who had bought their cars on hire purchase, to default on payments.

The firm was rescued by a major reorganization which took place under the guidance of two giant Japanese banks, the Mitsui and Tokai. The company was split in two parts, a production division (the Toyota Motor Company), and a marketing division (Toyota Sales Company). The scheme saved the company by providing working capital for the manufacturing division. The capital came from 'sales' of Toyota cars to the marketing company, the sales being paid for with bills which the Bank of Japan agreed to discount.

Since that time, Toyota has grown almost without check. It is the largest car producer in Japan, and Japan with a growth rate of twenty per cent in recent years, is the fastest-developing car market in the industrialized world. In the US market imports of Toyota cars have expanded without check since 1962. In 1966, 20,000 Toyotas were absorbed by the US market; in 1969, 125,000. This has made Toyota the only company except Volkswagen to sell over 100,000 in the USA in a single year; in 1969 Toyota accounted for a record eleven per cent of all new cars imported into the USA. It has now outdistanced its European rivals in the USA: Fiat, Volkswagen, Renault and British Leyland.

Toyota, the world's fastest-growing major car producer, sells about one-quarter of its total production abroad. This makes it Japan's largest single earner of foreign currency, yet the company is considerably less dependent on exports than some of its European competitors. Some forty per cent of Fiat's output, and more than seventy per cent of Volkswagen's go abroad, which emphasizes the prosperity and buoyancy of Japan's home market. The main factor in Toyota's success is the general world prosperity which has continued for much of the post-war era. Moreover the overall Japanese economic growth rate has been exceptional, and this, coupled with a highly protected domestic market, has produced a fertile environment for the development of big business corporations. But Toyota has not merely been carried on a rising tide of prosperity; it has outpaced its rivals. On world markets Toyota cars have made inroads in a host of new territories. In Japan, Toyota has steadily increased its share of a growing market.

The key to Toyota's success lies apparently in the skills and fore-sight of its management. In areas such as market research, sales, production engineering, finance, and labour relations, the management has an outstanding record of success even by Japanese standards. Toyota, like all Japanese car firms, has no lengthy, stultifying tradition. The Japanese car industry did not begin until the 1930s, and it was not until the 1960s that they entered the stage of vast mass production. Initiative and flexibility have therefore been more encouraged than in the older-established industries. From the outset, Toyota looked abroad for ideas on styling and design. It was able to benefit from the West's lengthy pioneering, and adopt the most modern and successful technology. In addition, the adoption of Western styling and standards of luxury has meant that Japanese cars have become instantly accept-able in the major markets of the world. By contrast, the European and American industries are very old. Many have inherited traditions of production and management which at times have inhibited progress. Whether in time similar problems will arise in Japan is an intriguing, but as yet unanswerable question.

Toyota has grown not simply in size but in prosperity. In 1969

returns on investment amounted to 22.2 per cent, making Toyota the most profitable of all of the major motor companies. The return for General Motors was 17.18 per cent and for Nissan, 18.4 per cent. Toyota's productivity has also been the highest of any major company. In 1969, sales per employee amounted to forty-four thousand dollars, whereas for General Motors the figure was thirty thousand, Nissan twenty-four thousand and Volkswagen twenty thousand. Moreover, in recent years productivity has been increasing at an annual rate of between fifteen and twenty per cent.

Toyota's efficiency comes from a number of factors. One is the newness of its plant. All passenger cars built at the firm's huge Nagoya works, which has a labour force of over forty thousand, are made in plants opened since 1959. At the same time Toyota has readily adopted advanced production techniques, and computers are extensively used throughout all operations. Toyota also has an enviable record in labour relations, with major strikes virtually non-existent since 1959. To some extent the devotion shown by Toyota's workers to their firm is a characteristic of all Japanese industry, but once again Toyota has succeeded even better than other Japanese companies.

As for oil, steel and cars, so in most enterprises an outstanding individual has left his mark on his industry, and so on the world. Most great industries have their great figures. Certainly one such was William Hesketh Lever, whose soap enterprise formed the basis of what today is Europe's second biggest company, Unilever. And Unilever is one of the very few European companies which, in its own field, is larger than any American enterprise. The place of Unilever today is seen clearly in a table of chemical and pharmaceutical concerns.

William Lever was born in 1851, the son of a relatively prosperous wholesale grocer in Bolton, Lancashire. At the age of sixteen William began work in his father's shop, and the grocer's boy ultimately became one of the greatest and most successful business men Britain has produced. He was created Viscount Leverhulme of the Western Isles in 1925, shortly before his death. No common stamp other than the urge for success seems to unite the great industrialists. Lever, certainly, had little in common with Ford or Carnegie. He resembled Carnegie in his short stature, but that was all. Unusually, Lever had a brilliant and imaginative mind, and possessed intellectual qualities rare in the industrial world. He was austere and authoritarian,

OPPOSITE The Tokyo Stock Exchange, one of the symbols of Japan's remarkable economic growth since the Second World War.

and had a boundless energy and unflagging zeal for work. He slept little, seldom more than a couple of hours, and was usually hard at work by the time dawn broke. The boy became a partner in his father's firm at twenty-one, and then devoted himself for twelve years to developing the business. It is remarkable how long he remained in the grocery trade, which hardly provided an outlet for his many talents. But at thirty-three, he went into the soap business with his brother, laying the basis of a huge fortune and a giant enterprise. Thus, in 1884, Lever Brothers was founded.

Before Lever's time, soap was cut by grocers from long factory bars according to the wishes of the customer. Lever hit on the simple, brilliant principle (which revolutionized the selling of many products all over the world) of pre-packaging, branding and advertising the product. He cut the soap into tablets, and wrapped them individually in gaudy paper. He used the brand name 'Sunlight', and pushed his product with one of the most famous and successful advertisements in history. It showed a man staring at an advertising slogan, saying 'Why does a woman look old sooner than a man?' 'She wouldn't, if she used Sunlight Soap.' Soon women throughout the world were using Sunlight.

In 1888 Lever (his brother took little active part in the firm) started work on a huge soap factory and model workers' village in a depressing marsh across the Mersey from Liverpool. He called it Port Sunlight. Soon Sunlight was exported, and was also being manufactured in Switzerland, Australia, Canada, Belgium, France, the Netherlands, the USA and Germany. Lever began to safeguard and develop his own supplies of raw material. He bought land in the British Solomon Islands to plant coconut trees, and also obtained a concession in the Belgian Congo for planting oil palm trees. Already by 1917 the capital of Lever Brothers amounted to fifteen million pounds and by 1924 this had grown to fifty-seven million. This was a fertile period of remarkable growth. Lever sold margarine when the war prevented imports from Holland, he founded an important food chain called MacFisheries, bought a whaling company, and took over half a dozen major British soap, soap-flake, chemical, oil-cake, and candle companies. By 1920 Lever controlled more than three-quarters of the entire British soap business. Throughout his life Lever was always preoccupied with the social implications of his wealth. Coming, like so many other tycoons, from a religious background, Lever's conscience was troubled by his massive fortune. He was at pains

to justify himself and his many acquisitions and he developed Port
Sunlight as part of a profit-sharing with his workers. Lever was always
a responsible employer and was one of the first to introduce an eight-
hour working day for his workers.

The company Lever built up became the greatest corporation
outside the USA, operating in more places with a greater variety of
products than any other company in the world. It did not grow
organically, like Fords, but, like General Motors, mainly by
acquisition and merger. Lever sought constantly to expand his
enterprises, and bought out company after company. By the time of
his death in 1925, aged seventy-four, he had built a world soap
empire with a capital of nearly sixty million pounds. The very
concept of brand products led Levers to become one of the world's
biggest spenders on advertising, and names like Stork, Lux, Lifebuoy,
Rinso and Persil, not to mention Sunlight, became household words.
Lever always preferred to buy up competitors than to combine with
them, and for this reason never joined with the giant Dutch margarine
empire, although in many ways a combination had clear advantages for
both. After Lever's death his successors came to terms with the
Dutch concern, led by Auten Jurgens, and formed the immense
Lever Brothers and Unilever combine.

The last concerns worth singling out as the basis of modern big
business are the electrical and electronic enterprises. In this field the
leading five firms in the group are all American. The USA, indeed, has

Dr Anton Philips, founder
of the giant electrical
firm.

86

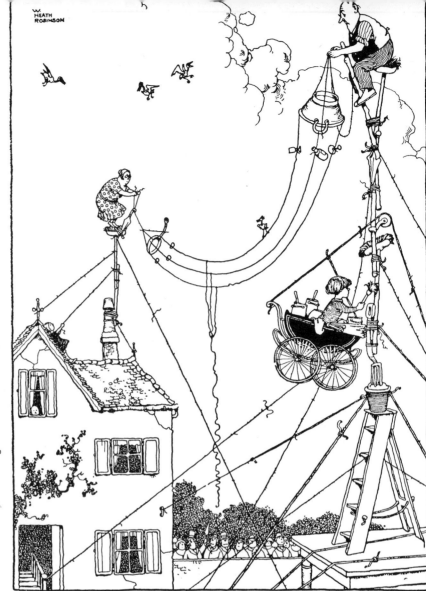

A Heath Robinson
cartoon illustrating the
difficulties encountered
by amateur radio enthu-
siasts in the twenties.

ten out of the top twenty. Japan has four, two are German and two
French. One is British and one, the biggest in Europe, is Dutch. When
we think about the manufacture of electrical appliances, we are likely
to think first of lighting, heating and the supply of electric equipment
to the home. Our communication systems, from the telephone to the
television set are based on electricity. We also realize that electric
devices have to be supplied for cars and aircraft. What is less
obvious, perhaps, is the progress of electronics – the science that
deals with the use of electrons emitted from solids or liquids and
made to move through a vacuum or gas – as, for example, in a neon
sign or a fluorescent lamp. The computer represents a more
sophisticated application of electronic science and one which has so

An early radio fan listens in to one of the first Philips sets.

far benefited the big organization. In the forefront has been IBM and the biggest European companies have had difficulty in gaining even a share of the market in their own countries. Japanese firms have been relatively more successful in this than AEG or Siemens in Germany, Philips in the Netherlands or Olivetti in Italy. The British firm ICL is holding its own with government support but the Americans have a considerable lead. The effect of the computer upon the business world will be discussed later, but the immediate point is that the electronic business is big in itself and of growing importance. We must also remember, though, that the giants depend upon smaller firms for their supplies of electronic components.

The attempt to group together the leading companies in different

One of the most international of all companies is Coca-Cola: ABOVE and OPPOSITE Coca-Cola advertising.

fields of enterprise makes for a measure of simplicity but leaves out companies of great importance which fall outside the categories chosen. Behind each great name lies a fascinating story. Major companies of international significance include two US aircraft giants, Boeing of Seattle and Lockheed of Burbank, California. Actually bigger than Lockheed are Eastman Kodak (whose founder shot himself), and International Harvester, which has recently bought the Dutch automobile firm Daf, with Caterpillar Tractor not too far behind. Sadly, we have ignored such famous companies as Singer, Xerox, Coca-Cola, Pepsi-Cola (probably the world's most widespread business) and Gillette – to which, so its rivals claim, the term 'cut-throat competition' was first applied. We have passed over

Bendix and Whirlpool and the British companies, Courtaulds, Rank-Hovis-McDougall and Cadbury-Schweppes. Even Nestlé, Switzerland's biggest enterprise, that giant food processing multinational, has fallen outside the confines of this necessarily limited survey. Nestlé dates back to a small Vevey chemist in 1865, and now controls Maggi soups, Findus frozen foods (jointly with J. Lyons and Co), Keiller's marmalade, Crosse and Blackwell's foods, Locatelli cheese, and others. Here, Swiss-like, even the managing director must clock in. There is no real end to a survey of big business. But enough has been said to show, in outline, what lies behind some of the household names. They were, in origin, very human institutions. The story of each reveals human failings and human achievements, desperate ventures and occasional folly, with the strangest mixture of foresight and luck. But once they became big, they changed. The sanctity of size put them in a different world, and they passed to a scale and diversity which their founders would regard with amazement and, quite possibly, with horror.

The Centro Pirelli
building in Italy.

3 THE INDUSTRIAL ESTABLISHMENT

The transformation from the heroic age to the period of the organization man has been swift. Great names survive to remind us of the founding fathers: Ford, Daimler, Siemens, Krupp, Philips, Dunlop, Cunard and many others.

Names apart, the present industrial establishment has much in common with the recent prehistoric age when the manufacturing mammoths first wandered the earth. Just as Rockefeller, Carnegie and Ford dealt in oil, steel and motor cars, so these three products continue to hold sway today. Other industries – rubber, chemicals, food processing and electronics – remain mere relatives, admittedly rich ones, but not of the blood royal. And just as all the three men were American, so big business continues to speak with an American accent. The world's ten largest companies are, with two exceptions, the USA's top ten, and of the top six enterprises three are oil companies. Indeed, the combined assets of the first five American enterprises are double that of the top five European concerns.

The motor industry must take second place to oil, even though General Motors comes first in size. Ford stands third and Chrysler seventh. By contrast, the top European firm, Volkswagen, lies only twentieth, Daimler-Benz comes thirty-third, Japan's Toyota and Nissan companies lie thirty-fourth and fortieth, while Fiat (50), British Leyland (54), Renault (55) and Citroen (106) lie far behind. In terms of assets the three American giants were more than eight times the size of the four principal European firms in 1972.

Electronics, the most rapidly expanding segment of big business enterprise, and chemicals are also characterized by the huge size of the leading firms. In electronics and electrical machinery all the main places are taken by US corporations. First comes the massive General Electric (not to be confused with the British concern of the same name) and IBM fifth and sixth in world ranks respectively. These are followed by International Tel and Tel (11), Western Electric (12), Westinghouse Electric (20) and RCA (25). Outside the USA, Philips (15) is the leader, followed by Siemens (24) and

Japan's fast-growing Hitachi enterprise (27). Others, such as AEG-Telefunken (55), Matsushita Electric Industries (56), Tokyo Shibaura Electric (60) and Britain's General Electric (71) fall a long way behind. In 1972 the sales of American General Electric exceeded those of the top three European companies combined.

In chemicals and pharmaceutical products, and also in the food industry, US pre-eminence is not quite so notable nor are the enterprises themselves of such formidable size. The leading chemical corporation is the old established US firm of du Pont de Nemours (24) in world rankings. But next, only two places behind, comes the British giant ICI. Another European, Germany's Farbwerke Hoechst comes next (30), with Italy's Montedison (34) following. Germany's BASF (36) just leads Proctor and Gamble (37), with Union Carbine (44) and the German Bayer company (56) next in world rankings.

In the food industry Unilever ranks first among all enterprises and is the world's ninth largest enterprise, Switzerland's Nestlé (28) comes next, followed by the US concerns Swift (45) and General Food (68).

These industries, oil, automobiles, electronics, chemicals and food processing, cover the largest of the world's enterprises. They account for the top twelve concerns in America, and the top fifteen in Europe. In Japan the biggest firm is an iron and steel giant Nippon Steel and this is fast challenging US Steel (19) as the largest iron and steel enterprise in the world. Other large firms are found in tyre manufacture, where America's Goodyear, ranked (27), leads, and in the aircraft industry, which, perhaps surprisingly, is only modestly represented in the world rankings. Boeing (42) is followed by Lockheed (51). No non-American firm is listed before Britain's Hawker-Siddeley Group (194) in the world and not even half the size of the USA's fourth concern, United Aircraft.

It is wrong to place too much emphasis on the exact place each company has in the list. Situations change rapidly and the sales figure itself may not even be the best indication of size. Ranking by assets would produce a very different order, while a comparison based upon the number of employees would produce a different order again: the oil companies, for instance, are not big employers in relation to their sales. Courtaulds (112) has a larger payroll than Standard Oil of New Jersey. Then again, mergers and acquisitions can considerably alter the ratings. Thus outside the USA the big French metallurgical company Pechiney Ugine Kuhlmann, formed of an amalgam of the forty-second and sixtieth ranked companies in 1972, now appears at

'*An aspirin, an aspirin, hasn't anybody got an aspirin?*' One impression of the takeover battle between giant chemical firms.

(27). Rapidly changing exchange rates, especially in recent years, have added to the purely statistical problems of international comparisons. When we classify companies by industry, we must always remember that their activities may be very diverse, and this highlights a problem which is becoming increasingly apparent, for with the rise of giant conglomerates it is difficult to say what products are characteristic of a given enterprise. Its output may well include a whole range. The twentieth-ranked concern in the USA in 1972 was Ling-Temco-Vought, a conglomerate with a vast and diverse range of interests. Outside America, Mitsubishi Heavy Industries ranks (17). It is not thought of primarily as an automobile company, although it makes and exports large quantities of cars, and, as well as being one of the world's largest ship-building concerns, it also builds aircraft.

Despite statistical dilemmas and verbal ambiguities, the bedrock of big business is clear. The giant concerns are found in a fairly narrow range of enterprise which includes oil, automobiles, electronics and to a lesser extent, chemicals, food products, steel and ship-building. And this feature is characteristic not only of the USA but also of most of the other industrial countries. In Britain oil is first, if we include Royal Dutch as part British, and third (BP), with Unilever (also Anglo-Dutch) second, ICI fourth, British Steel fifth, and British Leyland sixth. In France, as in Germany and the USA, an automobile enterprise, the state-owned Renault, leads. Next come the two metallurgical and chemical combines, Pechiney Ugine Kuhlmann and Rhone-Poulenc, the machinery firm of Saint-Gobain, and the oil enterprise Elf. In sixth place comes another car company, Citroen. In Germany the electrical equipment manufacturer, Siemens, follows Volkswagen, with the chemical concerns Farbwerke It Oechst and BASF third and fourth, and Daimler-Benz fifth. The sixth biggest German concern is the steel company August Thyssen-Hutte. In Japan, Nippon Steel is the biggest concern, followed by Hitachi (electronic equipment), Toyota, Mitsubishi Heavy Industry, and Nissan motors. While in the Netherlands the electrical giant Philips and the chemical combine Akso follow the two Anglo-Dutch concerns, Royal-Dutch and Unilever. In Italy Montedison (chemicals) comes first, followed by Fiat, Dunlop-Pirelli (an Anglo-Italian rubber and tyre enterprise) and ENI (petroleum products and chemicals). In Switzerland Nestlé is followed by Ciba-Geigy (chemicals), Brown Boveri (electrical equipment and machinery) and Hoffman-La Roche (pharmaceutical products).

These, then, are the biggest of the big. Others, household names, are indeed immense, but are not of the very first rank. It comes of something of a shock to realize that in the USA there are more than two hundred corporations bigger than Gillette, and over fifty bigger than Woolworths. Outside the USA some two hundred firms have sales greater than Britain's famous J. Lyons.

US supremacy, then, would come as no surprise to the nineteenth-century pioneers, but there is much that would not be so familiar to them today. For one thing, companies are now much bigger than they have ever been before, operating on a scale quite inconceivable to previous generations. Second, they have found a new way to grow, for whereas the founding fathers tended to expand organically – by concentrating and dominating in one particular product and market – today's giants are, as often as not, the result of mergers and amalgamations in widely diverse areas of manufacture. Third, whether they have their head office in the USA or not, this is the age of the multinational company, whose interests and activities can offer a real challenge to governments. Fourth, there is the rise of Japan, which is already beginning to alter the traditional balance of industrial power.

The takeover boom in the USA and Britain began soon after the Second World War and was intensified from 1960. One aspect of this movement was the appearance of the conglomerate. Holding companies had existed from earlier times but these had financial control over industrial concerns which were at least in roughly the same line of business. There now appeared holding companies which had bought control of totally unrelated enterprises. The origin of this fashion is to be found, no doubt, in US anti-trust legislation. Hindered from expansion in their own field of enterprise, some corporations expanded into other fields.

But other motives came into play, bargain-hunting being one of them, and the result was the conglomerate. In considering this phenomenon we must rule out the financiers who have gone from one business to another. The late Mr Joseph Kennedy was at different times a banker, shipyard executive, stockbroker, film magnate, real estate operator and owner of Chicago's Merchandise Mart. Howard Hughes has been film magnate, aircraft manufacturer, hotel owner and much else, but neither he nor Kennedy tried to organize their contrasting activities simultaneously and through one and the same holding company. That is the peculiarity which distinguishes the

Two of the few pictures taken of the elusive Howard Hughes. In this photograph taken *c.* 1937, he is seen talking to Lockheed's chief sales executive. In 1938, with a crew of four, he flew a Lockheed aircraft around the world in a record-setting 3 day, 19 hour journey – a triumph of precise navigation that Hughes emphasized on his return 'was in no way a stunt'.

conglomerate kings, and a glance at the list of leading companies will be enough to convince us that these men are or have been important. Further study of their activities will reveal, however, that they are or were financiers rather than industrialists.

In the list of US industrial corporations published by *Fortune* in 1970 there appear the giants we expect to see from General Motors and Standard Oil (NJ) down to US Steel, Westinghouse and Standard Oil of California. But after that, listed fifteenth, comes Ling-Temco-Vought. At thirty-sixth, after North American Rockwell, comes Litton Industries, and at fifty-fifth comes Rapid-American. Gulf & Western comes sixty-fifth after Consolidated Foods, and Textron stands sixty-sixth, ahead of Coca-Cola. Teledyne is placed at ninety-sixth and Olin at a hundred-and-sixth. These are some of the conglomerates and our surprise is to find them so high in the list. How does Ling-Temco-Vought appear at fifteenth and even at fourteenth the year before? It is arguable that the world's first conglomerate is the Japanese House of Mitsui, which became a joint-stock company in 1911, with divisions engaged in banking,

Howard Hughes with Ginger Rogers.

mining, warehousing, paper manufacture, ironworking, drapery and shipping. It may be doubted, however, whether Americans were aware of this. The story in the USA begins, therefore, albeit tentatively, with the merger of Olin Industries and Mathiesen Chemical in 1954, a merger itself preceded by Mathiesen's acquisition of E. R. Squibb, the drug firm, in 1952. Olin Mathiesen, as the new group was called, needed reorganization and consolidation. There followed instead some further acquisitions of a daunting diversity:

It had been manufacturing what was probably the widest assortment of products of any corporation in the USA, among them industrial chemicals and agricultural chemicals, brass and aluminium, cigarette paper, cellophane, flashlight batteries, Winchester guns and Winchester-Western ammunition, hardwood flooring and lumber, anti-freezes and brake fluids, explosives and power-actuated tools, nuclear fuel elements and high-energy fuels, Squibb drugs and pharmaceuticals. To be sure, a policy of diversification has served many companies well. But the trouble at Olin Mathiesen was that its fifty-odd plants and enterprises were never effectively co-ordinated.[1]

This is putting it mildly for it is on record that its thirty-six research chiefs never even met before 1958. The corporation was in trouble before that, its recovery beginning from the date when Stanley Osborne became president in 1957. He sold off or closed down some of the plants and reduced the number of divisions from fourteen to seven. He made a workable federation out of what had been a 'loose confederation of tribal chieftains' with interests divided between irrigation and aircraft, between insurance and scent. He was able to see good results by about 1964.

There was warning enough in this example, one might think, to have discouraged others from following the same path. But one who refused to be discouraged was Charles B. ('Tex') Thornton, who acquired Litton Industries in 1953. It was then a small firm manufacturing microwave tubes but it presently comprised 188 plants in thirty-one states and twenty-four countries which produce nine thousand products, of which half were unknown five years ago. These products are varied enough but a number of them have in common that they are sold to the defence branch of the US Government. It is no surprise, therefore, that this Texan's empire should centre upon Los Angeles. It comprised fifty other corporations by 1965 with products varying from typewriters to nuclear submarines, from calculating machines to frozen foods. To maintain some sort of rule over this amorphous empire Thornton relied and relies upon modern systems of analysis and control. There are some inherent difficulties, however, as evidenced by the fact that Thornton spends, it is said, four hours a day on the telephone.

There was a bad period for Litton Industries in 1967 but the company recovered next year and has since been called the fastest-growing organization in US business history. Diverse as Litton's interests may be, they have at least a similarity in their technical complexity and recent development. In Thornton's words, 'We have never acquired companies as such. We have bought time, a market, a product line, a plant, a research team, a sales force. It would take us years to duplicate all this from scratch.'

Thornton's chief rival in the conglomerate world is James Ling of Ling-Temco-Vought, centred not in California but in Dallas. Ling began in electrical engineering, moved into electronics and is involved, like Litton and on an even larger scale, with control systems and missiles, with aircraft and sports equipment. Another vast conglomerate is hidden behind the demure title of International

Telephone and Telegraph, a group mostly devoted (before 1959) to the manufacture of telephone equipment. Under the leadership of Harold Geneen the group has since acquired such diverse interests as Sheraton Hotels, Continental Bakeries, Avis hire-cars and Bols-Merrill publishers. Other conglomerate chiefs include Charles Bluhdorn of Gulf & Western, Fred Sullivan of Walter Kidde & Co, Henry Singleton of Teledyne and Rupert Thompson of Textron.

So far the conglomerates have been mainly confined to the USA. They are not characteristic of British industry and still less characteristic of the European scene. It would be wrong, however, to conclude that conglomerates are unknown in Britain or indeed in Europe. They have often resulted, where they exist, from efforts to diversify, as for example when the demand is vanishing for the company's original and main product. The Forestal Land & Timber Co thus produced material for leather tanning and had to look elsewhere when synthetic leather appeared on the market. It acquired some companies engaged in metal plating, in the manufacture of paint driers, animal feeding stuffs and health foods. When the company was bought out, however, by Jim Slater in 1969, the new board disposed of many of its assets. It is true that the Slater Walker group

Jim Slater, the British self-made millionaire who, like so many others before him, finds little more to do with his ready cash other than donate it to charities. Slater, an ardent amateur chess-player, doubled the financial prize at the World Chess Championship match in 1972 between Fischer and Spassky. His offer of £5,000 to the next British player to become a grandmaster is still open. Some people, however, criticize the methods he used to accumulate his wealth.

is something of a conglomerate but it is probably true to say that there is no British equivalent to Litton Industries or LTV; nor have other countries the Sherman Act which occasioned the conglomerate movement in the USA.

Let us look now at one of the chief preoccupations of the modern business man, the development of the merger, which follows the formation of the conglomerate.

Hardly a month passes without news of some major new amalgamation involving huge business corporations, either in Europe or in the USA and scarcely a week goes by without some smaller merger, or at least the rumour of one, setting off a fever of stock market speculation. Mergers are part and parcel of the world of big business. Corporation managers, big and small, spend much time seeking out other companies to absorb, warding off attacks on their own stock, or carrying out the lengthy, complex, secret and highly rewarding negotiations that result in the formal proposal. Merchant banks prosper on their takings from mergers they promote, and management consultants, specializing in finding suitable mates for the yearning giants, are in constant demand.

It is a fact that the big companies are growing bigger, and also a fact that more expand by merger than by organic growth. In the USA, under the watchful, suspicious eye of the Department of Justice, mergers have nonetheless reshaped the corporate scene since the Second World War. In Europe also, where governments are generally less hostile, and even perhaps approve of them, mergers have begun to reshape the structure of business enterprise. Old names have disappeared, or become simply appendages to another concern, continued for goodwill but no longer independent. Austin and Morris, Cadburys and Frys, Packard and Studebaker, all once competing, have now teamed together.

The spate of mergers in the last twenty years forms the third great period of merger promotion in industrial history. At the close of the last century came the upsurge of the giant trusts in the USA with their smaller equivalents in Britain and Germany. In the 1920s came a further fever, again spearheaded in the USA, when the giant Chrysler group was put together. European monsters like Unilever took shape at the same time. Then, since 1946 has come the steady growth in the size of the corporations, which has waned at times, but soon revived. Europe, as well as the USA, is playing its full part in this current trend.

A merger may be accepted willingly on both sides, or it may be only technically a matter of agreement, the smaller firm having been bullied into surrender. A merger can also be the result of a takeover bid, a process which requires explanation. One has to remember, first of all, that companies were originally owned, as a rule, by closely knit groups of shareholders, related to each other by birth, familiar to each other as neighbours and all more or less involved in the same industry. This is the pattern of family firms, still characteristic of French enterprise and investment. Where the concern is larger, however, and its shares placed on the market, the shareholders can be more numerous than the employees. They are so scattered, moreover, that they probably have no active or concerted interest in the company's business. Their sole concern is in the price of the share and the amount of the dividend. To them the attraction of the shares is to be expressed by their price/earnings ratio (or P/E). What, they ask, is the actual return on the investment? In point of fact the P/E ratio can vary sharply between one company and another. There are old well-established and respectable companies which pay a conservative dividend, their shares being quoted at ten to fifteen times the value of their current earnings per share. There are other companies, by contrast, with a record of rapid growth over their short period of existence, whose shares sell at thirty to forty times their earnings per share. If a company with a shorter history but a higher P/E ratio makes an offer to the shareholders of a company with a lower ratio, the bargain can be a good one: four dollars for three, say, in market values. The shares offered can be fewer, however, and if the combined organization should have the same earning capacity as its dominant partner had before, the dividend can be increased and the value of the shares will rise. This process can be repeated each time the opportunity presents itself and does not even imply any startling improvement in the quality of management. There is also the further possibility of offering the shareholders a debenture of higher face value in respect of each share previously held, a policy which will relieve the company of paying tax on that part of its earnings. Because of these known possibilities any company managed on conservative lines with a low P/E ratio is vulnerable. Some other and more ruthless company may acquire fifty-one per cent of the shares and vote its directors off the board.

The takeover bid, and especially a general awareness that such a bid is possible, may serve a useful purpose. It can also prove destructive,

Starting young in business
according to some
opinions, gives one a
distinct advantage over
one's rivals.

however, and that in more ways than one. First, it can replace
an old-established board of directors by new men of dubious
character whose sole aim is to take a quick profit and sell. This sort of
process can at once upset the world of big business and bring it into
disrepute. If one solid corporation has been successfully undermined,
which of the others can we regard as safe? Second, a takeover bid can
create unemployment. Some previously unknown group secures
control of a mammoth hotel in the city centre. It then announces
that the hotel is to be demolished and the site developed for office
accommodation. All the employees of the hotel are thrown out of
work and the city loses an amenity which is important to its
business life. A cinema chain is similarly bought for its site values and
with comparable loss to the community. A shipping line is acquired
by another group of financiers. But are the new directors interested

in ships at all? Perhaps their policy will be to sell the ships as scrap metal and develop the site of head office.

In many of these instances we sense that the old directors felt a moral responsibility towards their employees and towards the community while their supplanters feel no responsibility towards anyone. The result of this apparent contrast in motivation may be political interference – an official enquiry, a court order or the refusal of a permit. There may be questions asked in the legislature and sternly worded leaders in the financial press. Discussion may follow of possible legislation under which certain practices may be made criminal. The final result may be that the takeover bid is withdrawn and its originators are made to feel that they have stepped out of line. In extreme cases they can be made to feel very small indeed.

In the majority of cases the takeover bid would seem to succeed but the situation is sometimes complicated by the fact that one bid is eclipsed by another. A good example of this was provided by the fall of Odham's Press in 1962. The background to this drama was provided by the advent of commercial television in 1955. Newspaper circulation figures had been falling since 1950 but women's magazines had gained a useful share of consumer advertising. With the switch of advertising to television the weaker newspapers were soon in trouble. Weakest of them was Odham's Press which published the left-wing *Daily Herald* on weekdays and *The People* on Sundays. Its magazines were more prosperous and it also acquired those published by George Newnes.

The other and more flourishing newspapers were divided into several groups, one of them headed by Cecil King of the *Daily Mirror* and *Sunday Pictorial*, another by Roy Thomson, who had acquired the *Sunday Times* and ceased publication of the *Sunday Graphic*, these and others being formerly owned by Lord Kemsley. In January 1961 Roy Thomson proposed a merger of Thomson Newspapers and Odham's Press. The immediate result was a counter-bid from Mr King with a higher offer for the shares, an offer which the directors of Odham's refused. Mr King then improved his offer and the majority of the shareholders agreed to accept it. What King was aiming to secure was something like a monopoly of the women's magazines. Roy Thomson (now Lord Thomson of Fleet) countered smartly by acquiring a controlling interest in Illustrated Newspapers (the *Tatler* and *Bystander* etc). This was a part

DU PONT'S COPELAND

of the process by which two dominant newspaper groups have come into existence, largely sharing a dwindling advertisement market. The weaker newspapers, including the *News Chronicle*, *The Star*, *Empire News* and *Sunday Graphic*, have disappeared and the surviving groups have acquired a considerable investment in television. *The News of the World* nearly fell to a bid from Robert Maxwell of Pergamon Press in 1969 but was thwarted by Rupert Murdoch of the *Melbourne Herald*. The balance of power is far from stable even now, as was presently shown by Cecil King's own fall from power.

Undoubtedly mergers, involving the predatory capture of old concerns and the disappearance of hallowed, familiar names, have contributed to public fear and suspicion of big business. Also, concern for national prestige is aroused by international mergers, for anxiety about foreign control of domestic subsidiaries is very real. Earlier merger movements were very different, and to some extent the fears of monopoly and evil business practices that still colour attitudes today have their roots in the older movements to which the present mergers bear little resemblance.

Between 1890 and 1904 came the first major merger movement in US history, between Standard Oil of Ohio, United States Steel and du Pont's chemicals, who were the largest of the new giants. The

The du Ponts of Wilmington. FAR LEFT President Jefferson (*right*) suggests to the first du Pont, Eleuthère Irénée that he should start a powder mill. ABOVE Eleven du Ponts attend a board meeting in 1957. OPPOSITE RIGHT One of them, Henry, provides the cover for *Time* magazine.

corporations of this period were relatively straightforward: they were trusts, or holding companies, pieced together by bankers, to monopolize, or at least dominate, markets. The trusts were fully integrated, monster corporations, and they resulted in a more fully monopolized market within US industry than has ever been seen since. Today, by contrast, no merger is ever negotiated with complete monopoly in view. Competition may be narrowed between the giants, but it is never abolished. Nor have the tactics of the earlier giants been repeated in our own time.

The second great merger movement in US history lasted from the end of the First World War until the great stock market collapse of 1929. As in the 1890s, the large banking houses were again instrumental in promoting and financing the mergers. The new enterprises were floated on the crest of the wave of speculation that flooded the USA in this period. Corporations were merged to provide new securities for a public crazed with the desire to buy in Wall Street. And, as in all speculative fevers, there was opportunity in plenty for fraud and corruption as a naïve public parted readily with its savings. Too late were the evils of many of the mergers discovered. Congressional hearings, dragging on for a decade, uncovered fraud after fraud. Especially in the sales of public utility stock, the giant financiers like the Insulls and Hopsons, and the bankers who worked with them, mercilessly robbed the investing public.

The more recent industrial mergers, by contrast, taking place under stricter legal controls, have seldom been the work of financiers. Nor to any great extent have they resulted in the formation of new holding companies. Rather, they have been initiated by the operating executives of industry itself, using the services of bankers and middle men on a fixed fee or small percentage basis instead of involving the financiers as direct participants.

Why do firms merge? The most powerful motive is to promote growth. In an age of rapid economic expansion most firms seek at least to keep pace with the general growth of the economy. Few are content with their market share. Moreover the overall growth of a market means that individual firms must also expand, even if only to retain no more than their own share of the market.

Given the imperative of growth, mergers are a quick, cheap method of expansion. If a firm can absorb another, use its assets more productively, and take advantage of the internal economies generated by size, then the merger will result in improved profitability and a faster rate of growth. As well as economic incentives for growth, the personal ambitions of the men who control the giants also promote expansion. The industrial imperialist, out to lead an ever-developing corporation, finds in merger the quickest way to expand. No great company is without a whole string of mergers in its history. No great industrial leader of recent times has not had ambitions to build up his territory.

The resulting mergers have produced mammoth concerns with widely differing complexions. Some mergers are vertical, when a corporation extends its operations upwards to the finishing and marketing of products, or downwards to secure the raw material base for its operations. Others are horizontal, when a corporation expands by merging with other enterprises competing in a similar range of products. And there is also the relatively new phenomenon, the conglomerate, which encompasses many widely differing operations.

The more successful a company is in a single field, the faster is it likely to reach the limits of its growth. Even if it dominates a market, it may become static if the market itself does not continue growing. This stimulates constant efforts by the big corporations to widen their markets, by advertising, improving their products, and entering foreign markets. Such efforts also stimulate diversification. Numerous firms expand into related fields by merger, in order to make use of their own expert knowledge, experience and organization, and the reputation attached to their name. Continental Can, for example, has moved away radically from making straightforward, simple metal cans, and now has very large interests in all types of containers, and in plastics. It has extended its operations largely through merger.

Thus, just as the overall growth of a corporation is integrally related to its mergers, so is its diversification. Both are major forces in the modern business world. Mergers, moreover, beget other mergers. A company which absorbs many others, often finds wholly new markets opened up to it, and this promotes further mergers. A corporation which merges vertically to ensure its raw material supplies may well find those raw materials useful in other fields. The movement of Unilever from soap to palm oil plantations, thence into margarine, and ultimately into union with the Dutch margarine interests, is only the most conspicuous among many examples.

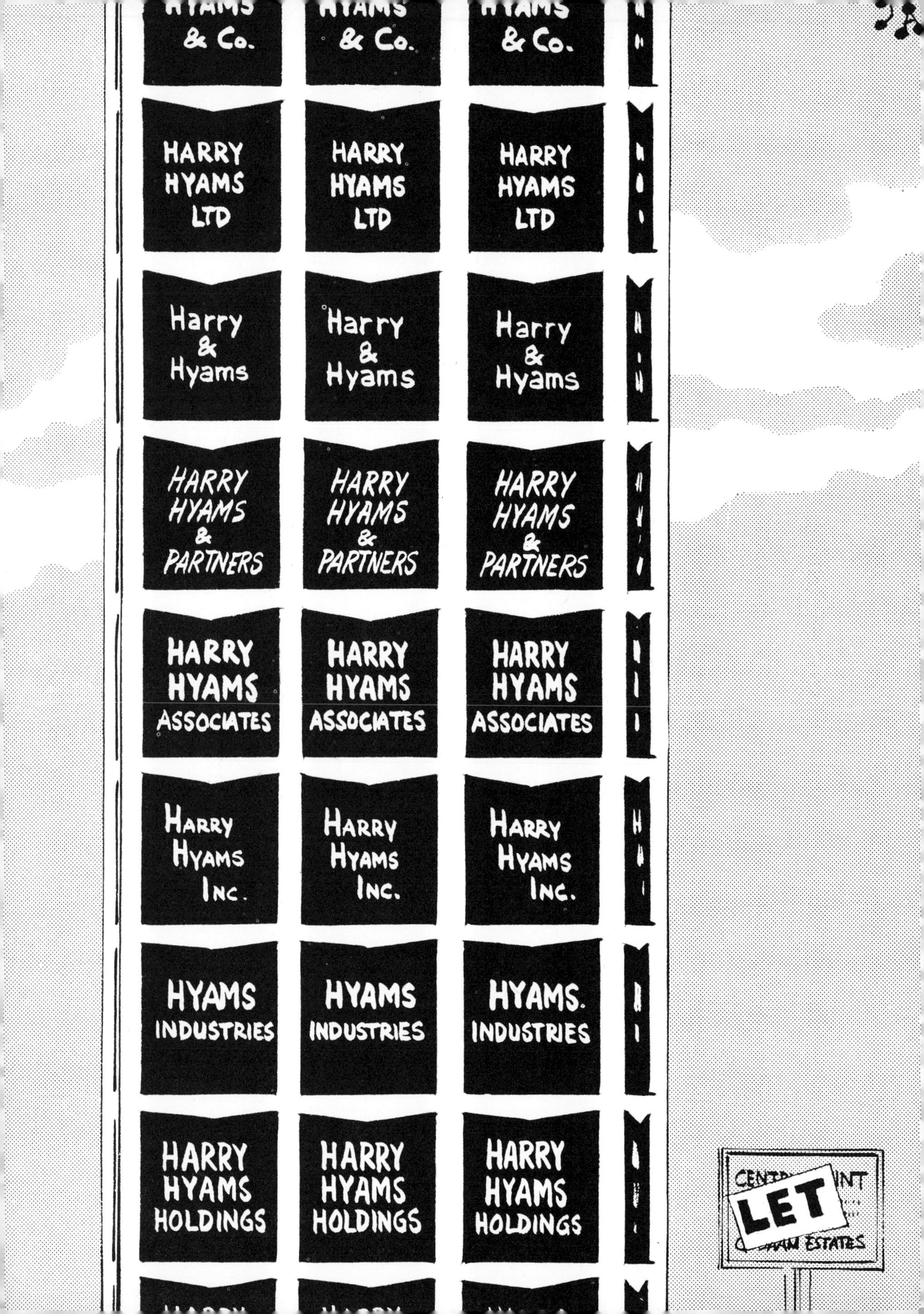

The conglomerate merger, on the other hand, is a new phenomenon. Starting in the 1950s with mergers among small businesses working in dissimilar fields, conglomerates have now definitely entered the field of big business in the USA. To some extent the conglomerate is a protective device by small and medium-sized firms to ward off takeovers by large companies. Banded together, small businesses feel safe. They gain the advantages of size, which eases the problem of finding capital for expansion, while larger capitalization itself reduces the numbers of potential predators. Indeed in today's business world small and medium-sized businesses are often potential targets for takeover by ambitious larger concerns, because they may well be under-capitalized. And stagnant firms too are in danger since financial difficulties may expose them to attack.

But the conglomerate is also the product of another trend, one which may increasingly influence the structure of big business not only in the USA but throughout the world. The huge strides made recently in management techniques in the use of computers for controlling operations and reaching scientifically based investment decisions, and the new advanced methods of financial co-ordination, have led to large economies on the administrative side of business. In other words, the savings through large-scale enterprise have increased more rapidly in the administrative areas than on the production side. And so a firm with diverse products but with centralized control, accounting and marketing systems may be highly efficient.

The advantages businesses win simply by operating on a large scale are of course numerous. For one thing, large enterprises can afford the risks involved in development projects, and these tend to advance in step with the progress of modern technology. Nothing illustrates the problem more clearly than the disastrous failure of Ford's Edsel car, introduced in the USA in 1957. Rarely has a mass-produced car so totally failed to impress the motoring public. Less than one-quarter of the hoped-for sales target of two hundred thousand vehicles a year was achieved, and output had to be scaled down drastically. Fords lost a fortune, probably about eighty million dollars. Yet the corporation carried a loss which would have spelled bankruptcy for most others, continued to expand, and remains today one of the most flourishing corporate giants in the world. By contrast, the failure of the Jowett Jupiter in 1953, which resulted in a loss far smaller than that involved in the Edsel débâcle, led to the immediate insolvency and disappearance of the Jowett company.

OPPOSITE Cartoonist's satirical view of how giant companies protect their own interests. Centre Point, the vast Central London office block built by property developer Harry Hyams has remained empty since it was built over eight years ago – something which in view of London's critical housing situation has aroused widespread anger.

Size, moreover, and the wealth it can command, gives the corporation opportunities for more extensive technical research, more exacting studies of market opportunities, and a better chance to take advantage of the most up-to-date technology which often tends to be the most expensive. And of course, the economies of large-scale production are a constant factor in the desire of corporations to expand their operations, and hence to merge with other concerns as a means of achieving these economies.

The drive to grow has thus been a powerful force in the creation of mergers. Another factor has been the volatility of the market. Shifts in consumer tastes may threaten a firm which specializes in one product or in a narrow range of goods. Particularly with the immense growth of prosperity in the western world, rapid changes in taste, often brought about by fast-developing technology, have resulted. Even the firmest-established companies have to guard against their traditional products becoming obsolete. And safety is often sought by merger into newly growing fields, where both firms may have much to gain. A large producer of electric appliances, for example, with a widespread distribution network, may use its existing system to sell the product – colour television – of a company it has just acquired. Once more, security as well as profit will result from diversity.

Growing industries expand by merger, but declines too may stimulate amalgamation. History is full of examples. The depressed 1930s in Britain saw a pronounced trend among the once buoyant cotton textile, ship-building and coal-mining enterprises, faced as they were with over-capacity and high unit costs, to gain strength through combination. A similar tendency in the USA was stimulated by Roosevelt's administration under the New Deal codes. Even within thriving industries economics often inexorably foster concentration. For example, in 1953 there were six major independent motor companies in the USA outside the 'Big Three', General Motors, Fords and Chrysler. In 1954 there were only three. Now only one remains. In Britain not one British-owned rival to British Leyland exists, whereas Morris and Austin once had a score of competitors.

There are clearly many advantages in size, but these should not blind us to its drawbacks. Some of the biggest concerns suffer from the stultifying bureaucracy that tends to afflict all large organizations. Over-centralization is one problem. Frustrated managers of outlying subsidiaries may be unable to interest an out-of-touch head office in developing new and exciting projects. At the other end of the

The British shareholder is not dead.

Just forgotten.

"In the Seventies, there may well have to be a more active relationship between management and shareholders than there has been for many years. Management will no doubt adapt itself and form new ties with shareholders just as it has seen the need for doing so with government and with employees: gradually, sometimes reluctantly, but in the end quite positively and often very successfully."

(General Manager,
Central Planning Department,
FISONS LIMITED)

"Plop". Through the letterbox and onto the mat comes the Annual Report. Six sheets of difficult figures and an up-lifting speech from the chairman. And that's it for another six months. That's what company shareholder relations *shouldn't* be like. But sadly, they often are.

At Fisons (and we don't for a second pretend that we're the only people that think this way) we're determined that shareholders should really feel like someone who owns a part of the company; which is what this ad. is about. Indeed it's what most of the advertisements in this issue of The Times are about. They are a statement   for the benefit of share-holders, employees, customers, friends and anyone else who might conceivably be interested   about what Fisons are, where Fisons are going, and what Fisons stand for.

If, as you pass amongst this unprecedented array of advertising, you get rid of your impression that Fisons are just a great big fertilizer company, well and good. Once upon a time such a description might have been well-merited   but

not any more. And a good thing too. Chill winds have a habit of blowing on one-product companies, no matter how in-dustrious their workers or how energetic their management. Which is one reason why sixty-odd fertilizer manufacturers went out of business in the sixties; and why Fisons have taken good care to establish themselves strongly in many other fields of endeavour in the past ten years.

But diversity of operation does raise other issues. In particular it raises for all companies the fascinating question of corporate identity: what exactly *is* the business you are in? At Fisons, we've found our identity and have no doubt at all but that we are in the health business   human health, animal health and plant health. You will find examples of these activities in the pages that follow and although the treatment is light the subject is serious. Fisons are not, repeat not, and never again will be just a great big fertilizer company. Fisons are a vital new force in the international pharmaceutical industry with some immaculate products to their credit; a

brand leader in several consumer markets including the home garden and hair care; an aggressive international company in the field of crop protection products. And in the midst of all this diversity, the fertilizer division remains the amiable giant it has always been.

If you are a Fisons stockholder, then this is your concern, for in the end you are the arbiters of managerial performance. In the past stockholders tended to live a little in the dark about the nature of the business in which their money was invested and seldom spoke or voted unless there was a crisis. Such reticence is becoming rare today and by the end of the present decade it will be looked on as quaint. So if you want to know more about Fisons, read on.

The giant pharmaceutical firm of Fisons, in May 1970, bought up almost every display advertising space in *The Times* in a concentrated effort to contact their shareholders. One of their full page ads included a nude model, which generated con-siderable controversy since never before had *The Times* printed a picture of a nude.

scale, though, too loose an organization can lead to countless inefficiencies, with different branches of the same firm competing with each other. There may even be ignorance in head office about the exact overall performance of the company. Mergers too carry their own dangers. When one company absorbs another it takes over its management and distribution system, which can easily lead to wasteful duplication of activities. And hasty pruning of the new branch can have bad results. Mergers frequently produce bad feeling and low morale among employees on account of the inevitable changes in promotion prospects and job functions.

Multinational companies are, of course, one of the most obvious manifestations of the scope of present-day big business.[2] Since the Second World War one of the major developments in the business world has been the growth of giant international corporations which cannot truly be identified with any one country. Operating throughout the world, they employ people of many nationalities, and they transfer huge sums of capital between different countries in a variety of currencies. Thus Nestlé cannot truly be thought of as Swiss, nor Coca-Cola as American. Their products are not made in one country and exported to others, but are manufactured in many different countries and marketed through world-wide distribution networks. The same is true of the oil products of Shell and Standard Oil, Hoechst chemicals, Philips electric products and a host of others. The big multinationals are indeed huge. Several have annual sales as big as the national incomes of the smaller European nations, and their growth rates are much faster. The total sales of General Motors in 1969 was more than twenty-four billion dollars – greater than the Gross National Product of Belgium or Switzerland. Fords, with nearly fifteen billion dollars was larger than that of Denmark or Austria. Details of the extent of the major international companies' foreign enterprises are difficult to find, but it is probable that the assets of companies held outside their own countries amount to well over £60,000 million.

Multinationals are usually thought of as being American in origin. Certainly more are American than any other nationality, but the American share of all international direct investment is no greater than two-thirds, and some of the leading multinationals have headquarters outside the USA. Such are the Anglo-Dutch combines Shell and Unilever, Canadian Alcan, Swedish SKF, Italian Olivetti, German Hoechst and Swiss Nestlé. It is interesting that the larger

Japanese firms have as yet played little part in the field of multinational enterprise.

In a sense, though, it is wrong to regard the multinationals as being identified with any particular country. They are controlled as one corporate entity, with head office as the nerve centre. Varying degrees of autonomy may be given to subsidiaries by individual companies, but the overall interest of the corporation, transcending national boundaries, is the first priority. And this is what gives to the multinational its peculiar political significance, for international considerations may conflict with national. International companies can influence exchange rates by moving funds from one currency to another, and they can affect the balance of payments of individual nations by altering the prices at which goods move from one subsidiary to another. They can switch export orders from plants in one country to those in another, and their investment decisions influence national growth rates.

The multinationals have thus created new problems, and their rapid growth in recent decades has led to increasing public concern about their activities. To some extent the whole field of international economic relations is in a state of flux. For centuries, foreign trade was the main force behind the growth of the international economy, but since the Second World War there has been a change of historic significance. International production, rather than the export of products across national frontiers, has become of increasing importance. Indeed, far more goods are manufactured by US subsidiaries abroad for sales in those and other countries than are exported directly from the USA.

The international company itself, however, is not new. As early as 1670 the Hudson's Bay Company was founded in Britain to combine English capital and Scottish skill in establishing trading posts on the northern fringes of colonial America. These posts sold a wide variety of products to the Eskimo and the Red Indians including blankets, tobacco, fish hooks, metal cooking pots and guns. In return the company received beaver pelts for sale in Europe. Today, the Hudson's Bay Company still exists as a large chain of retail stores in America, and is still a British corporation controlled and directed from London. Thus, international production has a long history. Even earlier, moreover, the great European financial houses had extended their operations in many countries. In the Middle Ages the great Florentine banking enterprise of the Medici was operating branches in Rome, Lyons, Bruges and London. Yet until our own century cases of multinational enterprise have remained scattered and often impermanent. Only at the very close of the nineteenth century did the first of the modern multinationals appear. The first major US subsidiary in Canada was founded in 1876, when the large gunpowder trust of du Pont bought two gunpowder mills, thus starting its career as a major international concern. A few years later, in 1883, a branch of the American Edison company was opened in Canada. It later became Canadian General Electric.

On a much greater scale were the operations of Alfred Nobel, the Swedish inventor of dynamite. The obvious problems of transporting explosives encouraged Nobel to develop a scattered, rather than a centralized system of production. In 1866 he and others were already

An early photograph of Alfred Nobel (1833–96), the Swedish inventor of dynamite, at the age of thirty.

deeply involved in international production and marketing, and since the end of the war the movement has greatly accelerated. Many of the earlier corporations expanded internationally in order to secure supplies of raw materials, one of the main historical driving forces behind the growth of the multinational firm, although the spreading of risk, tax considerations and the capture of new markets were also important factors. In Canada, international companies dominate the long-established nickel-mining and forest product industries, as well as the newer oil and iron ore enterprises, while Unilever controls supplies of palm oil in Africa, Nestlé supplies of cocoa beans in Africa and Latin America, the oil companies sources of crude oil in the Middle East, and so on. But since the Second World War the strongest force behind international expansion has been the pursuit

Alfred Nobel in 1893, three years before his death. Appalled by the destructive uses to which his invention had been put, he used his fantastic personal fortune to finance the Nobel prizes – given for outstanding services to peace and the advancement of the arts or sciences.

of markets rather than the control of supplies of raw materials. Increasingly, the new multinationals produce similar products simultaneously in several different countries. In other words growth has become horizontal, rather than vertical as formerly.

Horizontal growth has undoubtedly been stimulated by the multiplication of independent nations in recent decades. The birth of new countries has meant an increasing variety of tariffs, company laws and taxation, which means that it is administratively easier and economically more rational for companies to operate within the areas of their markets. Also, with the growing sophistication of products and the development of consumer tastes, has come the need for local packaging and labelling services and the provision of stocks and spare parts.

Most international of all companies, judged by the number (84) of countries in which it operates, is Pepsi-Cola. Next to it stands Bata, the shoe manufacturers of Canada (originally Czechoslovakia) whose score is 73, easily beating Philips (light bulbs) and Unilever (soap). Other companies with a widespread organization are the chemical firms, Pfizer, CIBA and Palmolive-Colgate, Singer and Necchi (sewing machines), and the computer manufacturers, IBM, National Cash Register and Burroughs. The list should also include Gillette, Metal Box, Caterpillar Tractor, Bowaters (paper) and Cinzano.

If Pepsi-Cola heads the list it might be because the main ingredient of its product is water, a fact which might well incline the manufacturers to ship the other ingredients and do the bottling near each centre of distribution. One hesitates even to ask whether the same reasoning applies to Cinzano. More important than the companies named, and even more international in their outlook, are the oil companies of the world. As each oil field is a wasting asset, liable to run dry after a given period and often sited in a country which is politically unstable, the aim of these organizations has been to spread the risk. So far from relying on any one source of supply, the oil companies are continually seeking new territory. No one of them has any sort of monopoly but they are often forced to co-operate in situations of special complexity and hazard. If there is ever to be any effective world organization it will be the oil companies which will have done most to bring it about.

Already by the end of the nineteenth century the USA was the greatest industrial power in the world, and had outstripped all rivals in the development of modern technology and advanced forms of corporation organization. At the end of the First World War the USA was unquestionably the richest nation in the world, and US industrial firms had a huge and prosperous home market in which to develop and grow. With an assured base for expansion at home, and with a technology in advance of international competitors, the giant US corporations naturally sought to profit abroad from their knowledge, experience, and resources of finance and capital. Nor was it unnatural that Canada, a neighbouring country with vast but unexploited natural wealth, should provide the nearest focus for the USA's transnational effort. By the 1870s US firms had taken root in Canada. Today, more than half of all long-term investment in Canada is in foreign-controlled business enterprises, and many Canadian firms are seventy-five per cent to a hundred per cent controlled by foreign – mostly US – interests. Early experience in Canada was valuable to internationally minded US corporations, and they soon began to expand elsewhere. A further factor encouraging foreign enterprise in Canada was the development of tariff protection. A high tariff in 1879 encouraged a number of foreign firms to set up in Canada in order to take advantage of the net of tariff protection. Not only in Canada, but in numerous other countries from the late nineteenth century until the present day, tariffs and other barriers to international trade have been a potent force in stimulating the expansion of the multinational corporation.

Multinational corporations have also extended their activities in order to ensure some stability in the overall development of their markets. Just as concentration on one or two products can bring the dangers of over-commitment, so international concerns often seek to avoid over-dependence on one or two foreign centres. For example, a company might find its foreign-held assets nationalized; or its earning might suddenly be hit by devaluation, or suffer because of tariffs or new tax laws. But the multinational today usually disperses investment over as wide an area as possible in order to spread the risks involved. In this way the corporation aims at long-term growth and a steady expansion, rather than a short-term and possibly very rapid gain.

Multinational enterprise can take many forms. Some companies simply make arrangements with foreign firms operating in similar fields to lease patents or trade marks in return for a royalty or similar payment. Sometimes competing giants set up jointly owned

Hardly in the same league
as the du Ponts, Ford,
Rockefellers or Carnegie,
Hugh Hefner has never-
theless made a modest
crust out of his magazine
Playboy, and the other
trappings of his organization such as the Playboy
clubs. He is photographed
here with one of his
'bunnies'.

subsidiaries in a third market, as did US du Ponts and British ICI with Canadian Industries Ltd, though this was dissolved by the US Federal government in 1952 for contravening the Sherman Anti-Trust legislation. Again, favourable tax concessions often encourage the establishment of international holding companies in a particular country. Switzerland, for instance, encourages such companies by generous treatment of profits collected in Switzerland for remission abroad. The Swiss themselves actually control two of the most successful international business enterprises, Ciba and Nestlé, the latter being Switzerland's biggest concern. Like Switzerland, Canada's tax laws make it an attractive setting for international holding companies, while Liechtenstein and Panama have even more liberal laws and contain the headquarters of many large corporations financed primarily from outside their boundaries. The most usual form of multinational enterprise is, of course, the wholly owned subsidiary, and the unfavourable du Pont-ICI ruling of 1952 has certainly strengthened this trend for American companies. Firms like Kodak, Colgate, Gillette, and IBM export not only their capital and brand names, but also their organization and marketing methods, and, not infrequently, some of their most promising executives.

Multinational business has long aroused suspicion and fear. Many nations, especially the poorer ones, have seen direct investment as a means of 'economic colonialism', with the rich nations exploiting the poor. Foreign firms are thus frequently singled out for special attack during outbursts of nationalist emotion, and numerous governments have taken over the assets of foreign-controlled enterprises, imposed harsh new taxes, and restricted the remitting of profits abroad. Somewhat paradoxically, complaints are rather frequent that the giant multinationals concentrate their investment in other advanced countries, so helping them prosper to the detriment of the poorer nations. In fact, about two-thirds of all direct international investment is concentrated in the advanced nations with Western Europe taking pride of place, and only one-third in underdeveloped countries.

Multinationals bring obvious benefits in the form of improved and more varied products, with opportunities of employment, and vast new resources of capital. But they have brought, too, grave political problems, and not only to underdeveloped countries. During the last decade there has been mounting opposition in Europe to the

Playboy goes public: the February 1971 'Playmate of the Month' was the first contemporary nude to grace a stock certificate. It is not yet known whether Hefner proposes to donate his fortune to charity.

great US multinationals, and a number of countries have taken active steps to curb the growing inroads made by US companies on European economic life. In 1967 Jean-Jacques Servan-Schreiber wrote that within fifteen years, 'the world's third largest industrial power, just after the USA and Russia, will not be Europe, but American industry in Europe'.[3] The basic fear is that a country's economic sovereignty is threatened by the 'foreign' multinationals. By their actions, dictated by interests other than those of the nations where they operate, they can influence exchange rates by moving funds from one currency to another, affect a nation's balance of payments, undermine credit policies of governments, and even sabotage the employment policies of individual countries.

Undoubtedly, then, the multinational is a growing force in world economy. But just how important is trans-national enterprise to the corporate giants? Rather surprisingly, detailed statistics on many issues are lacking, Even the total extent of multinational enterprise remains largely a matter of speculation. Data for US corporates for the early 1960s, however, makes it clear that multinational enterprise looms large in the operations of many concerns. In the field of computers, for example, the foreign operations of Burroughs, IBM and the National Cash Register corporations accounted for fifty-four per cent, thirty per cent and sixty per cent respectively of their total profits. Black and Decker, to take another example, the leading firm in small power-driven tools, owed one-third of its total profits to activity abroad. A similar picture emerges over a wide range of industry. In pharmaceutical products both the large Pfizer chain and Schering medicines made some forty per cent of their profits abroad, while in the cosmetic industry Cheseborough-Ponds earned fifty-seven per cent, Gillette forty per cent, and Colgate-Palmolive sixty per cent abroad. In food processing, as much as eighty per cent of Heinz's 1960 profit of $8.7 million came from foreign operations, and for Coca-Cola the figure was forty per cent. For vehicles, Ford's foreign profits amounted to seventy-two million dollars in 1960, which was about sixteen per cent of the total; the largest tyre manufacturer, Goodyear, earned thirty per cent of its profits outside the USA, while Standard Oil of New Jersey earned two-thirds.

The importance of foreign operations for companies outside the USA is also hard to assess because of the lack of statistics. Philips, Ciba, Nestlé and Unilever must all have made a very large proportion of their total profits out of overseas business. Among British firms, it is known that the Metal Box Company, a British associate of Continental Can, made thirty-three per cent abroad, and the Bowater paper group seventy per cent. The Italian firm of Cinzano made sixty-six per cent of its profits outside Italy.

So far we have considered the profits of multinationals. Sales figures, too, give an impressive reflection of the importance of foreign activity. In the USA, one quarter of Ford's total sales come from operations abroad, while for Singer the figure is sixty-one per cent, Caterpillar Tractor thirty-seven per cent, Eastman Kodak twenty per cent, and International Harvester thirty-five per cent.

Some of the big international corporations concentrate their overseas efforts into a few areas, but others are represented throughout the world. The most important of the latter is Pepsi-Cola, which operates in more than eighty separate countries. Other widely dispersed multinationals include Bata, the remarkable Canadian-based shoe corporation, which before the Second World War was a Czechoslovakian concern and now operates in some seventy-three countries. Both Philips and Unilever are represented in more than fifty countries, IBM in thirty-six, and Colgate in thirty. Standard Oil, British American Tobacco, Ciba, General Electric, Kodak, Pfizer and Dunlop are also widely dispersed, operating in between twenty-five and thirty countries.

The emphasis in this book is on big business in industry, but the picture would not be complete without mention of big business in finance. Industrial and financial enterprises are closely interlocked. The epic story of Andrew Carnegie must include J.P. Morgan. What sense would the Toyota history make without some reference to Mitsui and Tokai? Industrial expansion is more or less impossible without money. It is usually the industrialist's second task to go where the money is. Having defined his aim he has next to find the means.

For the sake of lucidity it will serve our present purpose to divide financial agencies into three groups: the established institutions, the merchant banks and the freelance operators. It is a question whether these categories are really separate, for the historical trend is towards the respectability of standardization. Mayer Rothschild began as a pawnbroker, he and his sons being noted for transactions which would be unthinkable today in the offices of N.M. Rothschild & Sons of St Swithin's Lane. It is quite possible, therefore, that some financial houses now regarded as dubious will end as pillars

'*Do you think they know
something we don't?*'
A cartoonist's view of
international money-
lending.

of the financial establishment. Granted, however, that this trend exists we can still draw a distinction between those who are striving and those who have arrived. We must remember, moreover, that commerce comes before industry and that finance comes before commerce. It was the financier who often made the growth of industry possible.

In addition to the financial institutions mentioned above, which operate on a world-wide scale, there are the building societies in Britain. These were formed in Victorian England to collect subscriptions from their members and then to advance money on the security of the houses which members would build or buy. In doing this they have to comply with the provisions of the Building Society Acts of 1879 and 1894. These societies were at first small and unimportant for the Victorians rented their homes as a rule and had no great desire to own them. But when legislation was passed to protect the tenant, making eviction difficult or impossible, the owning of house property became unprofitable and would-be tenants were forced, in effect, to buy.

In 1913 there were well over fifteen hundred building societies, and between them they lent during the year about nine hundred thousand pounds. In 1935 there were under a thousand societies; but they lent over a hundred and thirty thousand pounds. The building society had become, from a position of comparative unimportance, the foremost investment agency in Great Britain. By the end of 1939 the British public owed the building societies seven hundred million pounds and in 1938 the societies made £137 million of new mortgage advances.[4]

Home-ownership finance was a familiar type of US business from early times but the boom came in California after the Second World War. The population drift was westwards towards a better climate and towards a land of opportunity. California also represented the final frontier where the westward movement had to stop. Land values there were bound to rise and property was the ideal investment. Southern California is the home of the new technology, which has taken the place there of motion pictures and oil. Around the new areas of industrial development there is, inevitably, a building boom. This is made possible, in turn, by the savings-and-loan firms (known as S & Ls):

The institution of the S & L is not a Southern Californian invention, but it has burst into its finest flowering there. In essence, an S & L is a specialized bank that attracts savings by offering higher interest rates than do the commercial banks and lends the money out to citizens who want to buy houses or to developers who want to build houses. . . . The postwar building boom in Southern California has turned several S & L's into multibillion dollar enterprises.[5]

One such enterprise Home Savings & Loan was headed by its founder, Howard Ahmanson, whose personal fortune was said to total something between a quarter and half a billion dollars. Born 1906, he was one of the men (Paul Getty and Joseph Kennedy being among the others) who foresaw the crash of 1929 and sold out in time. He is also perceptive enough to have remarked 'the only way you can have democracy is to have inflation'. He died in 1968, being until then the leader in this field of enterprise. His successor in the leadership of the S & L business is Sydney Mark Taper, a Polish Jew, born in England, who came to the USA in 1939 and bought the Whittier Building & Loan Association in 1950. He is now the founder, chairman and president of the First Charter Financial Corporation which has over two billion dollars in assets. A more colourful leader in this field was Bart Lytton, a former screenwriter who formed the Lytton Financial Corporation in 1959 (not to be confused with Litton Industries), a finance house with assets at one time of nearly a billion dollars which in turn controlled two S & Ls. His style, it has been said, was not calculated to endear him to the rest of the financial community. Nor was it calculated to perpetuate his legend indefinitely. After a first setback in 1965, when he was compelled to part with the Beverly Hills S & L, he was finally made to resign from the board of Lytton Financial in 1968. While this ended his career in that field of enterprise – leaving him still a millionaire – it left the S & L business as flourishing as ever and as highly competitive.

Earlier in this century the wealthiest men in the world – Carnegie, Vanderbilt, Rockefeller or Krupp – stood at the head of great industries which are mostly still in existence. Oil magnates still exist but the successors of Carnegie and Krupp are salaried and professional managers, controlling groups which have become national institutions. Industries founded more recently are headed, in many instances, by white-coated technocrats, by men of mystery, by priests of the computer, and experts in accountancy. There is little place it would seem, in advanced technology for robber barons and ruthless warfare. One obstacle to this more picturesque career is to be found in the tax structure. Because of this and because of other more or less socialistic

legislation, the modern tycoon is more of a financier than an industrialist. In the world of finance, therefore, some of the world's wealthiest men are still operating in their own highly individual style.

The four richest Americans are supposed to be Howard Hughes, Paul Getty, H.L. Hunt and D.K. Ludwig. All are believed to control personal fortunes of a billion dollars or more. Of these four men, two – Hunt and Getty – base their fortunes on oil, and one (Ludwig) on the tankers which carry the oil under the historic and battle-torn flags of Liberia and Monrovia. It is these who come nearest to the older pattern of Rockefeller or Gulbenkian wealth, so much so that Ludwig has been called the last of the great entrepreneurs. He and Hunt have interests other than oil, Ludwig in real estate, citrus fruit and salt, Hunt in canneries and lumber. Getty is more single-minded (apart from collecting works of art), oil and money being his chief and almost his only interests. More romantic than the other three is the mysterious Howard Hughes, who has combined strident publicity with extreme reticence. From the Hughes Tool Company, which he inherited, Hughes went on to found (1934) the Hughes Aircraft Company and the airline that became TWA. His achievements

'This is your last chance, Irving. Go into the Bayshore Inn, tell 'em you're Jane Russell, and demand to see Howard Hughes.' A British cartoonist's comment during the famous case of the 'hoax biography' of Howard Hughes.

Charles Clore, the great
British property magnate
at the sixtieth anniversary
of his London store
Selfridges.

include a record flight round the world in 1938 and a period as owner of RKO, the film company. It remains strange that one whose close friends include Katherine Hepburn, Lana Turner and Ava Gardner should shun publicity to the point of having avoided press interviews since 1954.

The Europeans who come nearest to this income bracket are to be found, some of them, in Britain. One of the first to attract public notice was Charles Clore, who controlled Investment Registry as from 1948 and the Furness Shipbuilding Company of Middlesbrough from 1951. Next year, through Investment Registry, Mr Clore made a successful bid for J. Sears & Co (True-Form Boot Co) and its six hundred-shop subsidiary, Freeman, Hardy & Willis. Other acquisitions followed but Mr Clore was not the only operator to reckon with. There was Hugh Fraser of the House of Fraser, originally interested in retail drapery, who captured the John Barker group – which included Pontings and Derry & Toms – in 1957, and then went on to succeed in a takeover bid for the Harrods group, which included both Dickens & Jones and D.H. Evans.

There was also Harold Samuel of the Land Securities Investment Trust, whose interests were (and are) in real estate, and Isaac Wolfson of Great Universal Stores, a pioneer in the mail-order business and in hire-purchase, who launched a campaign in 1954 which added 350 retail outlets to its 870-shop clothing and furniture empire and ended, for the time being at least, with the acquisition of Hope Brothers. Later in recent history we have seen the rise of Jim Slater, who founded Slater Walker Securities in 1964 and has since become very powerful indeed. It was his subsidy which finally persuaded Fischer to play chess against Spassky the Russian grand master in 1972. In these British financial battles the takeover bid has provided the element of drama. It was little known in France before about 1962, when the alliances were formed between Renault and Peugeot, between Fiat and Citroen.

As from that period mergers have been frequent and a number of financiers have come to the fore, the great names including that of Antoine Riboud, chairman of Boussois-Souchon-Neuvesel (BSN) and its leader in the takeover of Saint-Gobain. But French industrialists tend to have a bureaucratic background like Pierre Dreyfus, the head of Renault. There is also the strong tradition of the French family firm, the sort of background from which Jean Monnet comes. This is the background of Marcel Boussac, the textile multi-millionaire,

Aristotle Socrates Onassis
seen here with a
somewhat unresponsive
Princess Grace of
Monaco.

owner of fifty factories employing twenty-five thousand workers and
recording an annual turnover of over a hundred million pounds. He
also owns a chain of retail stores and the fashion house of Dior, which
he founded in 1947. To this empire he has added his own bank, his
own insurance company and the reputation which he derives from the
turf, having at different times won the Oaks, the St Leger and the
Derby. Germany also has its tycoons, one of them being Axel Caesar
Springer, owner of *Die Welt* and *Bild Zeitung*, a German Northcliffe
or Beaverbrook. But Germany is also much dominated by the
family firm, that of Friedrich Krupp, the great steel firm at Essen,
remaining in private ownership until 1967.

Apart from that, German industry is largely dominated by the
'big three' commercial banks, the Deutsche Bank (led by Hermann
Abs), the Dresdner Bank and the Konmery Bank. Belgium is still
more dominated by its banks, the Société Générale being the biggest,
and it is only the newest industries (mostly controlled from outside
Belgium) which are independent of them. Outside both Europe and
the USA is Aristotle Socrates Onassis (born 1906), owner of a tanker
fleet numbering about seventy ships, under flags of convenience, who
is actually resident in Argentina or Monte Carlo. His interests
include Monte Carlo (the casino, the Opera House and five hotels)
and Olympic Airways, and he is one of the last multi-millionaires to

own a real luxury yacht, the *Christina*, of seventeen hundred tons, manned by a crew of forty. His marriage with the widow of President Kennedy would seem to put him in a different class from his former rival, Stavros Spyros Niarchos (born 1909), whose $2\frac{1}{4}$ million ton supertanker group is actually managed from London. They count among the wealthier members of the international set.

Returning again to the USA, the men there with fortunes of about half a billion dollars include John W. Mecom and Henry Crown. Mecom began by finding oil but went on to invest in real estate, plastics, hotels and fishmeal. Henry Crown of Chicago began as a building contractor and builders' merchant but went on to other enterprises which included, at one time, the purchase of the Empire State Building in New York. It was bought by Crown and his associates in 1951. Ending as the sole owner, having bought out the others, Crown sold it again in 1964 at a profit of fifty million dollars. Next to him, with over three hundred million dollars, comes W. Clement Stone who began as an insurance salesman and remained in that business, presently owning the Combined Insurance Company of America (Chicago), which has satellites in Dallas, Boston and Wisconsin, and in Canada, Australia and New Zealand. With a comparable fortune was the late Joseph P. Kennedy who became President of the Columbia Trust Company, went from there to the Bethlehem Steel Corporation, from that to the stockmarket and from there to the film industry.

Joseph H. Hirschorn is a former stockbroker who found uranium in Canada and ended with a fortune of about a hundred and fifty million dollars. A fortune of a hundred million dollars was made by Norton W. Simon, whose speciality has been in acquiring ill-managed companies and making them profitable by reorganization and new investment. He had made himself a multi-millionaire by the age of thirty-five. He has owned, at different times, Val Vita (orange juice), Hunt Brothers (tomato products), Ohio Match, Wesson Oil, Canada Dry and *Saturday Review*. Like Getty, Simon collects works of art. This too can be a speculation but Simon's collection is said to be very valuable indeed.

The background to much of the USA's more recent success story lies in the world of modern technology and more especially in the world of electronics, radio and television, the computer, defence systems and space exploration. The first computer was built by a group of Harvard and IBM scientists in 1944. The transistor was invented in the Bell Laboratories in 1948. As from these dates we have had a new type of industry with characteristics which need to be understood. The leaders in the new technology are seldom business men in the old sense. Some of them are, like Howard Hughes, but more of them are electrical engineers, physicists and graduates of the business school. They are today the brotherhood of the Ph.D, the salaried experts and key men of the present age. The electronic industries are located on principles which did not apply to the older factories. The transportation advantage which the midwest retains in component production and in automobiles is of dwindling interest to the new technologists. They demand a location which is near but not in a major city; a sunny climate which will be attractive to the sort of staff they aim to recruit; and they want an area blessed with reputable universities and good schools.

It is the proximity of well-equipped research laboratories which will allow them to strengthen their scientific staff, and the proximity of

A nineteenth-century view of a stockbroker. 'His means are in supposition.' – *The Merchant of Venice*.

good schools and universities which will enable them to retain the staff they have, tied to the area by their children's educational needs. The present industrial prosperity of the Los Angeles area owes something in this way to population and climate but as much again to the Los Angeles campus of the University of California (UCLA). Nor is it any coincidence that Texas Instruments (founded 1950) fixed their headquarters at Houston, or that Honeywell, since merged with GEs computer division, should have its main plant near Minneapolis. Where the scientific industrial complex is somewhat remote from existing centres of learning, as at Cape Kennedy, the new University has to be supplied, as in Florida's Atlantic campus. As against that, the most lavish educational facilities around Boston, which presumably attracted Transitron to that area, were insufficient to make up for the unpleasantness of the climate.

The basic formula for the new technology is thus to combine a sophisticated industry with good universities and schools in a pleasant climate near, but not in, a major centre of population. But this is not all because the picture, to be complete, needs a big injection of federal money, usually in the form of defence contracts. It is in this atmosphere that we see the new kind of industrial academic, often hired as part-time adviser by the new professional industrialist. They meet and mingle on the common ground of the jointly sponsored research programme and then again at the scientific conference and business convention.

Theirs is a well-paid existence in a stimulating atmosphere, spoilt only by knowledge of the fact that federal policies can change overnight and that federal funds may be cut off at the source. These dramatic changes in pressure are not due to demands for economy but to fluctuations of fashion. Last year's drive to utilize oil derivatives is merely the prelude to this year's fuss about ecology. The one thing we shall never obtain from democratic politics is continuity.

No account of big business would be complete which ignored the rise of the unit trust. Small investors wish to share in the profits which can be derived, as they know, from investment in equities. They are prevented from playing the market in this way, however, by three major obstacles. First, the shares often change hands in relatively large blocks. Second, the small investor is still less able to spread his risk among several kinds of stock. Third, he will probably realize that he lacks the knowledge of the market which will give him any prospect of success. It is the purpose of the unit trust to overcome those three difficulties. By accepting large sums made of small investments the directors of a unit trust can deal on a sufficiently large scale in a wide variety of shares and with the best obtainable advice. Any element of risk in any one share is offset by the diversity of the total investment and the caution with which most of the shares will have been bought. In this way the larger unit trusts can be regarded as big business. They are highly respectable and are guided by the most responsible advice. They are sponsored by eminent merchant bankers and offer both a fair dividend and the prospect of capital gains.

In Britain there are the investment trusts, the largest with an investment valued at £138,939,000, and eight others with assets of over £100 million. There are also the finance houses, those in Britain headed by the United Dominions Trust (with £209,897,000) and Lombard Banking (with £150,082,000). There are also a great number of companies engaged in hire-purchase finance and more again with their capital investment in property. Among all these impressive institutions there are bound to be some marginal examples of behaviour which is less than exemplary. As a reminder of this it seems appropriate to end this chapter with a short account of one such disaster and one in which a great many investors lost their money. Even in big business there must be the occasional failure and the bolder the climb the greater the fall.

One discovery of the mid-twentieth century is that small investors want to share not only in large-scale investment but (some of them) in large-scale speculation. The ordinary unit trusts, such as those listed, are not in any way speculative and are unlikely to produce a sensational, as opposed to a merely satisfactory, result. Some small investors want to aim high, not always realizing the risks they must inevitably run. To cater for this demand there have been some rather dubious enterprises, especially those operating 'off-shore', outside the legal system of the larger countries. The classic example of this is provided by the career of Bernard Cornfeld who began as a salesman for the Investors Planning Corporation. This was at a period when Jack R. Dreyfus of New York turned the Nesbett Fund, which he had bought, into the Dreyfus Fund registered in Panama. Valued at between two and three million dollars on 1 January 1955, it rose to between five and six million by the end of that year, an increase of 143 per cent. Knowing of this success, Cornfeld went to Paris where he presently set up as agent for Dreyfus.

... Cornfeld had made an interesting discovery. He had found that there were at least two types of Americans in Europe. There were the servicemen, who had reasonable quantities of money in their pockets, but who more and more frequently were accompanied by wives and children, which made them increasingly disinclined to blow all their pay on living it up.

And then there were the exiles. Today, large herds of gentle, conformist rebels against American culture graze anywhere in Europe they can find grass. In 1955, in Paris, Cornfeld was among the vanguard of the invasion. . . . It was a world of frustrated intellectuals, mild neurotics, political nonconformists and cultural misfits, with the occasional drunk or homosexual[6] . . . .

Cornfeld's inspiration was to make some of the exiles sell mutual funds to the servicemen. The plan succeeded but the French authorities proved obstructive. So Cornfeld went to Geneva, recruiting his sales force by means of the slogan 'Do you sincerely want to be rich?' From this new centre Cornfeld's syndicate, called Investors Overseas Service (IOS) sold fifty-eight million dollars' worth of Dreyfus shares in 1959.

Then Cornfeld created his own fund, the International Investment Trust (IIT), sponsored by banks in Switzerland and Holland, which

Bernie Cornfeld, who later claimed that his childhood in the streets of Brooklyn eminently suited him to be a philanthropist. He built up IOS until it had two billion dollars to invest. He is seen here in Geneva, where, on a visit to his aged mother, he was arrested by the aggrieved Swiss authorities, and put into jail, where he could muse on the dwindling of his 'Fund of Funds' to a mere five million dollars.

began operations in 1960 and had collected $3.4 million by the end of 1961. Cornfeld had no expert knowledge of investment, his skill being almost entirely in the recruitment and motivating of salesmen. His next idea was to launch a new IOS subsidiary to be called the Fund of Funds, proclaimed as a Fund formed to invest in Mutual Funds and registered in Ontario. It had collected $16.65 million by September 1963 and a hundred million by the end of 1964. Many other subsidiary companies were launched in the years to follow, sixty in Nassau alone. At this point some authorities took alarm and IOS was forbidden (1967) to trade in the USA. There was even trouble with Swiss work permits, which compelled Cornfeld to shift most of his head office staff (thirteen hundred of them) from Geneva to Ferney-Voltaire, just over the French border. There was further trouble with the police in Portugal, Colombia and Brazil. Rumour had it that IOS was handling some very hot money indeed and that further trouble was impending.

The time had come to improve the public image. Cornfeld did this by recruiting as directors James Roosevelt, Wilson Wyatt, Edward G. Brown (Governor of California), the Earl of Lonsdale, Sir Harmer Nicholls, Sir Eric Wyndham White and Count Carl Johan Bernadotte of Sweden. Rumour was quelled but the peculiar and complex structure of IOS gave these distinguished men no say whatever in its policy. The most useful name in this galaxy was that of Roosevelt, more revered in the world at large than in the USA. To young Germans of the post-war generation everything American was progressive and modern and IOS, with the Roosevelt name, was doubly attractive. Lacking any tradition of investment, they fell for IOS in a big way and had contributed $257 million by 1969. In that year the IOS executive had control of two billion dollars and boasted that they had the financial advice which such a sum would buy. That year they were riding high and investment money was still pouring in. As a tentative step, IOS offered for sale some of the shares in a subsidiary, IOS Management Ltd. Offered at $12.50, these shares stood at $180 by March 1969. This was indication enough of public confidence. There was, unfortunately, little basis for it.

IOS investments had never been particularly successful and the efforts made to justify the salesmen's optimism led its officers into wilder and wilder speculation. They had some measure of success in making capital gains on a rising market but what if the boom were to end? Later in 1969 IOS went public, offering eleven million shares at ten dollars each. Shares were sold to the value of $52,400,826 and the company's officers sold blocks of their own shares at the same time. More than eighty-seven of them became millionaires and Cornfeld himself had some fourteen million in cash as well as ninety million on paper. IOS shares, offered at ten dollars, rose briefly to fourteen and then began to decline in value. The whole stock market was falling and there was panic in the air. By April 1970 the price of IOS shares fell to $8.5, to $5.5 to $4 and ended as virtually unsaleable.

As for the Fund of Funds it practically ceased to exist from the investor's point of view. All that was left, after Cornfeld had left for Acapulco, was a terrifying thicket of inaccurate figures, dubious statements and legal complexities, with the vague possibility of some money still there at the bottom of the heap. The whole story gives us a disturbing idea of how completely the world can be fooled by the eloquence of salesmen, some perhaps deliberately cheating their clients but others, more dangerous, deceiving themselves. For a brief period IOS, with two billion dollars to invest, was clearly big business; a fact which business men will do well to remember. Of those who built up that house of cards the kindest thing that could be said was that they were blinded by greed.

The New York Stock
Exchange – a bird's-eye
view.

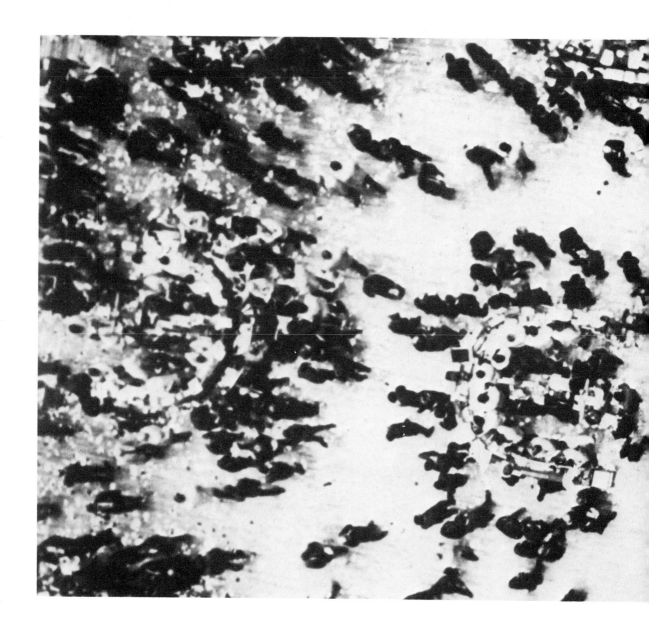

4 METHOD AND MADNESS

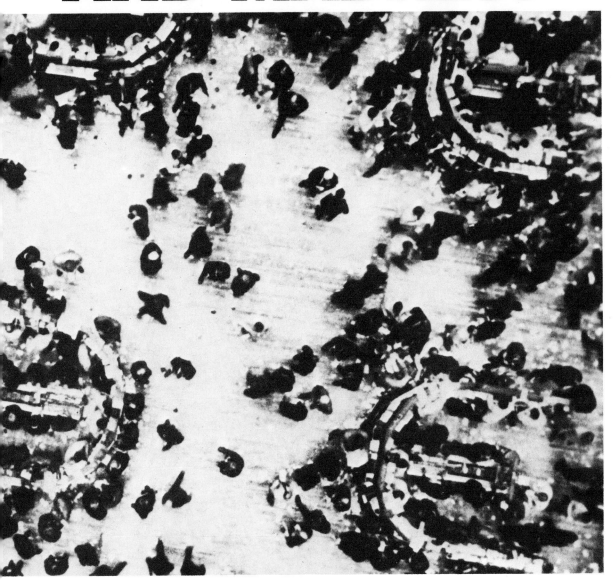

Most big businesses were founded by a man of unusual ability or even genius, whose talents and opportunities coincided at the right moment of history. We think at once of James B. Duke, Cyrus McCormick, William Clark, John D. Rockefeller, Henry C. Frick and Henry Ford. Recalling what we know of these giants we realize that usually they united ownership with a strong personal control. In their early days they ventured all they possessed. Later in life they had a fortune at risk and could have lost all by a single wrong decision. They were and they had to be men of courage. They had the advantage, however, of being in a position to make controlling decisions and were not compelled to justify themselves except in terms of success. They could act where others might have had to argue. The result was that their personal staff was often a mere handful. Many a leading industrialist carried all necessary information in his own head, scribbled financial calculations with his own hand and issued orders with his own voice. The great Marcus Samuel, for example, the founder of Shell, was head of two companies in 1901 (Marcus Samuel & Co and Shell itself) which shared the same headquarters in Leadenhall Street. The total of the combined staffs came to forty-eight, including four male typists in the private office and five lady typists who worked for the other departments. Harvey S. Firestone similarly owned and ran his own company with little assistance from anyone else. The late Lord Marks, founder of Marks and Spencer, the retail chain (with a turnover of £165 million in 1961) worked from a relatively small office in Baker Street. We learn of Marcel Boussac, the French multi-millionaire, that he personally directs his business down to the last detail:

He conducts his business from his offices in the Rue Poissonière in Paris, which are quite remarkable in their simplicity and lack of ostentation; M. Boussac is not a man who cares for spending money on appearances. In his office M. Boussac sits behind a huge Empire desk, on which stands a remarkably old-fashioned telephone but none of the other elaborate mechanical contraptions which are fashionable today among

business executives; and there, for the greater part of the year, with very few holidays, he carries an appallingly heavy burden of work, with a meticulousness which demands the highest degree of exactitude and precision in everything which is done either by him or for him.[1]

We have a rather similar picture of Paul Getty, whose oil empire (valued at perhaps four hundred million pounds) used to be run from a modest and untidy suite in the London Ritz where he answered his own telephone and dealt with his mail by means of a laconic scribble in the margin of the letters he received. This has been and still is the business style of many men who have founded and who own the organization they direct.

For a number of reasons, however, the founder's system is apt to die with him. His successor is usually a man of a very different calibre. The possible patterns of succession are broadly three. First, the founder can be succeeded by his son, his son-in-law, his brother or his nephew. Friedrich Krupp thus founded an industrial empire, which has remained in the family until quite recently and has been the property of a single owner. In the presidency of the Ford Motor Company, Henry Ford was succeeded by his son, Edsel Bryant Ford, and he in turn by Henry Ford ii. Examples of other more or less successful dynasties are provided by the Barings and Morgans, the Vanderbilts and Rockefellers. It may be doubted, however, whether any dynastic succession can last for very long. The son or grandson is seldom as capable as his great predecessor, nor is his

Big business requires rapid communications and fast transport – these in turn are big business. The Bullet train which runs between Osaka and Tokyo.

motivation likely to be the same. Why should the millionaire by inheritance work hard to make millions more? It may happen, as we know, for the second Vanderbilt made more than the first, but that is not the usual story. Family firms still flourish in Europe, however; Frederick J. Philips (son of the founder) was head of NV Philips Gloeilampen Fabriken until recently and then handed over to his brother-in-law at a time when annual sales reached $4.2 billion. All the stock of Henkel, the German makers of Persil and other chemical products, is still owned by forty-one members of the Henkel clan, and the present chairman, Dr Konrad Henkel, is grandson of the company's founder. Instances of this sort of continuity are less frequent in the USA and Britain. Granted a continuing family influence on du Pont, it more frequently happens in the USA that the family yields control while retaining ownership, but even this pattern is unlikely to be permanent. For one thing, those who live on investments do well to spread their interests widely and will be advised against holding a vast share in a single firm. For another, they may have expensive hobbies, like politics or taxpaying, which will compel them to sell. One way or another the moment must usually come when the firm and the family have to part.

There is also the danger of external attack, if an organization has become vulnerable and flabby. The attack often comes from an unexpected direction. Business is lost to a company which had not even been regarded as a competitor. A brewery can thus be undermined

by a maker of ice cream. Of this trend the classic example is provided by the railways. The founder of modern big business, the first US industrial millionaire, was Cornelius Vanderbilt (1794–1877) whose fortunes came to be based on the New York Central and the railway system which connected New York with Chicago. He was followed by the men who took the railway lines across the continent and nothing could have been more impressive than the railways of about 1900. Then they began to deteriorate, accumulating vast numbers of useless employees and resting on a monopoly position in many of the regions they were supposed to serve. But the inefficient railway was not killed by another railway. It was killed by the long-distance truck, the aircraft and the car. In the list of leading companies there is no mention today of any railway. Where railways once appeared we now see the names of General Motors, Ford, Boeing, Greyhound, Lockheed, Grumman, Carrier, Cessna and United Airlines. The railways were all but swept away by a new technology, and this is a danger to which established companies are still liable. In the more socialist countries like Britain and France the over-staffed railways are nationalized and run at a loss, their deficits being made good by taxpayers who travel by air.

We shall now examine the internal problems that a company may have to cope with as time passes. The founder's successor in office may be his ablest surviving colleague or partner, who may or may not be a major shareholder. This is another extension, as it were, of family control, as when Lord Marks was succeeded by his brother-in-law, Israel Sieff. But this again merely postpones the day when the company has to go public.

The third alternative is for the group to be sold during the founder's lifetime. The classic example of the founder thus relinquishing control was provided by Andrew Carnegie who sold in 1901 the group which then became the United States Steel Corporation. The purchasing syndicate was headed by J. Pierpoint Morgan but the final result was to spread the ownership of the corporation among 160,000 stock-holders, a third of them employed by the corporation itself. Whatever the previous history, the final picture is of the shares being widely distributed among the investing public. The new shareholders are broadly of two kinds: institutions and individuals. The institutions include merchant banks, insurance companies, unit trusts and other companies. The individuals may include some big financiers but most of them will be small investors scattered over the country and the world. As these small investors have no contact with each other they have little chance of forming a pressure group to influence policy. Their interest in the concern is limited to receiving (and sometimes grumbling about) a dividend. The point has been reached when ownership has been divorced from control.

It is at this point that theory and fact begin to disagree. We have always been told that the limited liability company is strictly controlled by its shareholders who come together at the AGM and elect, from among themselves, a board of directors. Once elected, the directors go on to elect, from among themselves, a chairman. Under his general guidance they go on to appoint the company's executive officers, who will be responsible to the board of directors and so, through them, to the shareholders. Nothing could be more democratic and proper, the whole procedure being faintly reminiscent of Parliament or Congress. Nor would fact be far from theory if the shareholders numbered only about fifty with all or most of them present at the AGM. But the shareholders actually number a hundred thousand (say), of which total some twenty are present, none of them with more than a trifling holding and none of them, presumably, with anything better to do. They are congratulated by the managing director on the success of their company, they are given copies of a beautiful report and their suggestions, if they make any, are received with rapt attention. In Kenneth Galbraith's words:

> Votes of thanks from women stockholders in print dresses owning ten shares . . . are received by the management with well-simulated gratitude. All present show stern disapproval of critics. No important stockholders are present. No decisions are taken. The annual meeting of the large American corporation is perhaps our most elaborate exercise in popular illusion.[2]

So far the facts given are broadly true of big companies in the USA or Britain and applicable to quite a few companies in Europe. But the companies themselves are not otherwise the same in structure and they need to be classified from the outset. In its simplified form the big corporation or company is one which has gained a position of dominance by a process of development and growth, expanding very often on the same site or at least in the same area. The Ford Motor Company is a leading example of this type, bearing the stamp of the founder's personality. Friedrich Krupp is much the same, a circle of plants round the head office at Essen. Big companies of this type will establish themselves in other countries, but their original pattern was a simple one and they are apt to retain some trace of it. A variation of this pattern results from vertical integration, the control established over sources of supply and also perhaps over trade outlets. Early examples of this structure are US Steel and Lever Brothers in Britain. Quite different is the organization which has grown by lateral expansion, the federal amalgamation of companies which were fairly similar in importance, no one completely overshadowing the rest. General Motors and EI du Pont de Nemours are the leading examples of this sort of structure, but Britain's ICI is much the same. Since the process of amalgamation was a corporate decision, it cannot be said that the final organization had a single founder. There is yet another type of company which has a central enterprise surrounded by subsidiary companies which have never been actually absorbed. The United States Rubber Company was at first an alliance of this sort and the Ericson Group of Sweden retains something of the same character. Their historical and national differences underline some of the current arguments about centralization and decentralization. This is a subject to which we shall return.

It is generally accepted that big business today, with control divorced from ownership, is coming to be run by professionals. The founder and his descendants go, and most of the present top executives are chosen for their skill and experience, not for their family influence or wealth. Many of them hold degrees in science or law, or qualifications in engineering or accountancy. The percentage of men so qualified is on the increase and so is the proportion of men with a degree in business administration. As long ago as 1945 this trend was pointed out in the USA:

> Summarizing the evidence that the leaders of big business are developing a profession of business administration, it should be noted first, that wealth and family position have declined in importance as a way to the top; second, that the amount of formal education expected has increased; third, that increasingly long years of experience are required before being entrusted with top positions; fourth, that the officials themselves are for the most part completely absorbed in their work; and, fifth, that a professional code of ethics is emerging.[3]

If this was the trend twenty years ago in the USA it has clearly not been reversed since, nor has it been confined to the USA. Management is nearly everywhere more professional, the exceptions being in the new sorts of enterprise which spring up unexpectedly outside the boundaries of established industry.

Professionalism in management was first studied by Frederick W. Taylor in 1882. He was a foreman at the Midivale plant of the Bethlehem Steel Company who devised time-and-motion study, which became Scientific Management in 1911 and led to the foundation of the Efficiency Society in 1912. Associated with him was the mathematician Carl G. Barth who is sometimes credited with the invention of the slide rule. This is untrue, because William Oughtred, rector of Aldbury made his slide rule in 1621, and another, dating from 1654 is still in existence. Nevertheless, the connection added a certain authority to Taylor's system. Scientific method began to be applied to manual work, and soon to management itself. One machine which made a great improvement was the cash register, sold widely in the USA from about 1895. From this developed the improved tabulating machine of 1919.

In the meanwhile, however, there was a spate of books written on management, published both in the USA and – by Sir Isaac Pitman & Sons – in Britain. As the books became available, it became easier to organize courses of study in commercial subjects. Then came the computer, invented in 1942 and gradually made available on a commercial scale. IBM's 701 machine became famous during the Korean war. By 1958 there were a thousand computers in use in the USA, and 160 in Europe. With the aid of this machine, management could properly be called a science, and with more confidence as computers have multiplied. There are many examples today of the managers wearing the white coat of the scientist and even a few examples of the scientist becoming a manager. With head office acquiring the solemn atmosphere of a research laboratory there can be no doubt that professional management has arrived.

There was from the outset a certain confusion about the terms in use. The word 'Efficiency' was used at first and came into popular use. The practitioners in Europe mostly called themselves Industrial Engineers, as they still do. Practitioners in the USA and Britain have come to be called management consultants. Under various names the consultant existed before the Second World War but the boom in consultation began after 1945. There are now about 2,700 consultant firms in the USA and another sixty accounting firms with a consultant division or subsidiary. There are said to be fifty thousand consultants in the USA earning between them about a billion dollars a year. Many of these are practising in a small way but the companies in big business will usually employ the big consultants, McKinsey, Booz Allen, Cresap McCormick or A.T. Kearney & Co, or else turn to the more specialized groups, Bruce Payne and Science Management (for cost-cutting) or Diebold (for computers). Cresap McCormick employ 175 consultants and collect about $8 million a year in fees.

Others work on a bigger scale although not necessarily on a higher level. Peat, Marwick, Mitchell & Co, one of the eight biggest accountant firms, has a consulting staff of a thousand earning thirty-five million dollars a year between them. When Booz Allen went public, offering its shares at twenty-four dollars, the two senior partners (Bowen and Allen himself) made six million dollars each and the most junior director 1.3 million. The firms have been going public as their founders reach retiring age, a trend which might seem inevitable, but concern has been expressed about consultant firms subsequently being bought up by industrial concerns and conglomerates. Could industrial secrets leak from the consultant to the owners of the consulting firm who might be the client's rivals? That may be more of a theoretical than an actual risk. The one certain trend is towards a higher degree of specialization. As corporations become more sophisticated, employing their own computer experts and forming their own organization-and-method departments, their need is less for the general consultant than for an expert (on occasion) in textile production, airport management or behavioural science.

Founder of the consulting business in Britain was Charles Bedaux (1886–1944), born in Paris but an early migrant to the USA where he founded a number of consulting firms. He has been described as 'eccentric, exhibitionistic, brilliantly original, impossible to work with, a spendthrift and a maker of fortunes'. His British Bedaux Company was formed in 1924 and eventually became Associated Industrial Consultants, its early members leaving to found their own firms. Urwick, Orr and Partners had begun business by 1934 – James Orr having worked for Bedaux – and Production Engineering Ltd dates from the same period. As in the USA the business expanded after 1945, the Management Consultant Association being founded in 1956. This did not include all consultants but it did include the bigger firms, Association Industrial Consultants Ltd, Personnel Administrators Ltd, Production-Engineering Ltd, and Urwick, Orr & Partners.

It was estimated in 1956 that there were about a thousand consultants in Britain, earning about four million pounds a year between them. The four larger firms employed eighty per cent of the consultants in 1961 and did eighty per cent of the consulting work. In 1971 the member firms of the MCA numbered twenty, eighteen with head offices in London, one near Manchester and one in Leeds. They have provincial and overseas branches, however, and do a great deal of work in India, Africa, Ceylon, Turkey and South America. The number of consultants employed by the member firms reached a peak in 1970 (3,200 with a twenty-nine million pound turnover) but declined somewhat in 1971. It is an interesting aspect of consultancy that it expands and contracts with the economy as a whole. The available figures suggest that firms call in expert advice when they have money to spare, not when their problems include a reduced cash flow. Consultants are evidently brought in more to help exploit opportunity than to avoid disaster.

In Europe the countries which list the highest number of consultants in proportion to population are Sweden, Norway, Denmark, France and the Netherlands. Many of these practise internationally, however, especially the Dutch, whose work extends to Germany and France. The countries which have so far offered the least scope are Italy, Germany and Finland. In Japan there are no consultants at all, apparently because the equivalent work is done by bankers. Germany had only 220 consultants in 1965 but their number had more than doubled by 1970. Alongside the consulting firms in Britain and elsewhere are the management recruitment firms. Their existence is a reflection of the shortage of trained and experienced managers, which is revealed still more dramatically by the newspaper space devoted to high-level notices of 'situations vacant'. These 'head-hunting' firms undertake to supply the needed talent, conducting their own tests and interviews and billing the employers, not the employed. Useful ancillaries in the same general field are the suppliers of temporary office help – Kelly Services, Manpower and Office Overload. These also act as work measurement specialists, not merely supplying the temporary personnel but advising the client what staff will be needed to perform a given task. Perhaps the simplest method of reducing the cost of overheads is to replace permanent by temporary staff, lessening the number in the off-peak periods and avoiding the cost of fringe benefits for the larger number which would otherwise be paid while idle.

Leaders of industry can also resort to the far cheaper method of obtaining advice – the reading of books on management. Early examples of these were F.W.Taylor's *Scientific Management* (1911), *The Modern Corporation and Private Property*, A.A. Berle, and G.C. Means (1932) and Dale Carnegie's *How to win friends and influence people* (1936). There followed *The Managerial Revolution* by J. Burnham (1945) and thereafter a flood of post-war literature. Books of obvious importance included *The Practice of Management* by Peter Drucker (1954), *The Organisation Man* by W.H.Whyte (1956), *The Hidden Persuaders* by Vance Packard (1957) and *The Affluent Society* by J.K. Galbraith. Books on management multiplied afresh after 1960 and the titles now seem numberless. One thing at once apparent is that few books of significance are written by the industrial leaders themselves. Possible exceptions are *A Business and its Beliefs* (i.e. IBM) by Thomas J. Watson (1963), *My Years with General Motors* by A.P. Sloan (1964) and *Up the Organisation* by Robert Townsend (1970). The fact remains, however, that the influential books have been mostly written by consultants, like Peter Drucker; by journalists, like Vance Packard; or by the occasional professor, like J.Kenneth Galbraith. The most perceptive comments

TOP (*left*) and (*right*) A cartoonist's opinion of management consultancy. BELOW J.K.Galbraith in thought. Professor Galbraith's books have greatly influenced the public attitude to big business.

have thus come from people not in business at all. It is these and a hundred other authors who have provided the business schools with books for their shelves and topics for their seminars. What influence the books have must remain a matter of guesswork and the same doubt surrounds the impact of the same men when they address a business conference. All we can say with certainty is that their ideas have been widely discussed and are known among the top executives of the biggest firms.

Come now to the schools of management. There was talk about the need for these from an early period of modern history but the idea ran contrary to the institution of apprenticeship and the secrecy which surrounded what the apprentice was supposed to learn. Daniel Defoe admittedly attended a dissenting academy at Newington Green where the syllabus laid stress on modern languages, geography and shorthand. It was long, however, before business administration became an accepted part of higher education.

The oldest business college in the USA is believed to be the Wharton School, founded in 1881 as a part of the University of Pennsylvania; a successful experiment rather ahead of its time. The real moment of breakthrough was represented, perhaps, by the foundation in 1909 of the Harvard School of Business Administration. Other US universities were quick to follow Harvard's lead but there was more reluctance in other countries; so much in Britain that little was done before 1960. It is true that the London School of Economics was founded in 1895 but its early bias was more towards public than business administration.

The demand for management training, except at the lower level in technical colleges and polytechnics, began after the Second World War. It was then, after the business schools were founded in London and Manchester, that the universities began to display a mild interest, some of them offering a degree and others a post-graduate diploma. It was argued at first in university circles that business management is too narrow a subject for undergraduates and that the better plan was for the graduate (in law or economics) to return to the university after having gained some business experience. That might be a good policy but the practical difficulties are soon obvious for a married man with children who has made himself indispensable to the firm for which he works.

The final answer has been in most cases to offer a degree course with, in addition, a three-months' course for graduates with business experience. There can be endless argument over the respective merits of general and specialist education and the answer may well be that there is room for both. Similar problems have been met in the European schools, Fontainebleau, Baden-Baden, IMEDE at Lausanne, CEI (Geneva) and St Gallen, but European and British undergraduates start with a better general education than is now readily obtainable in the USA.

Whether the future leaders of industry will be graduates of the business school is a question not easily answered. And at the same time it is not yet proved that scientific management, involving the use of computers and other scientific aids as well as the theoretical skills of business school graduates, is the best. In a recent and significant study of top management Dr George Copeman shows that firms with the fastest growth are not those headed by men specially qualified but those in which the chief executive owns a substantial share of the equity.[4] His survey suggests that the founders of now prosperous firms are generally more capable than their more professional competitors, having a clearer understanding of the situation, a quicker head for figures and a more confident approach to problems of finance. One realizes that the founder of a business has, in one way, a simpler task than his successor. He finds or creates a need for a certain product and then supplies that need up to saturation point. In creating

One view of an employer–employee attitude.

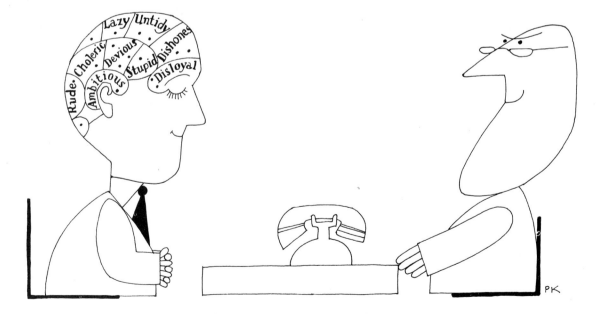

Disneyland the late Walt Disney, an unquestionable genius, left little for anyone else to do. This is often the situation when a company's founder retires or dies. His successor may well find it impossible to sustain the firm's growth rate. The fact that sales level off is no proof in itself that the new managing director is less competent than his predecessor. But we can suspect that the trained professional manager

'Let's have our little talk over here, Elliott, where neither of us will feel intimidated at my desk.' A cartoonist's view of authority.

is more likely to be sound than brilliant. He has been taught to avoid mistakes. He knows how to present and interpret a balance sheet. He is understandably reluctant to take risks with other people's money. These are useful habits but they are not necessarily accompanied by inspiration, and the avoidance of danger is not at all the same thing as the perception of opportunity. There is a further risk that scientific management can lose touch with human realities. The scientist knows that all molecules will behave in a certain way under given conditions. Placed in a position of authority he is tempted to assume that human beings are as predictable in their reaction to a situation. The more 'scientific' a manager becomes, the more remote he may be from his colleagues, employees and public. There can be no doubt that professional management will provide the answers to some problems, but it also creates its own.

If we turn from the science of management to the power politics of the company itself we soon realize that it is no different from any other organization, whether church, university, republic, army or club. It contains, like any human society, the elements of monarchy, aristocracy, nobility and democracy. In a very illuminating book[5] Antony Jay compares the modern corporation with the medieval kingdom. It is headed by a king (or president, or managing director) who is surrounded by his courtiers and advisers (directors and specialists) and who seeks to maintain his authority over his provinces, some near and some remote (divisions and subsidiaries), each immediately ruled by a baron (or plant manager) who may be either docile or turbulent and whose own authority (over his factory) may be effective or weak. It has been the fashion among liberal theorists to argue that progress means the process by which monarchy turns into aristocracy and that into democracy. There is nothing in history to support this. The truth would seem to be that patterns of rule follow a repetitive sequence and that the form adopted at a given period is chosen in response to a particular situation – a threatened frontier, a period of prosperity, an opportunity for conquest, an imminent revolt – and that the emphasis is changed as the situation alters. The basic elements are always there – the rule by one, by a few or by many – and the instinct of mankind is to prefer what seems appropriate to the given state of affairs. In the leading corporation or company the element of democracy, represented by the AGM is merely vestigial. This is for the same reason that it is becoming vestigial in politics; because the organization is too large and its problems too complex. Those who will admittedly have to pay for any failure (the voters or shareholders) are too numerous to be assembled and too ignorant to express an opinion. The competition for power is between the king, the courtiers and the barons. It is decided partly by situation and partly by personality and may well be influenced by a consensus of opinion among the troops themselves.

The underlying and often quite amiable conflict between courtiers and barons is represented today by the concept of staff and line management. At the elbow of the chief executive stand his chief advisers, originally the specialists in finance, production, marketing and law. To these have often been added the specialists in advertising, personnel management and research. Where the chief executive is uncertain of himself or lacking in prestige, his advisers are very important. It may be they who are making the decisions, perhaps after discussion among themselves, perhaps with only cursory reference to their nominal chief. Where the chief executive is strong and confident, by contrast, the advice offered him will be more tentative and he may well have acquired the trick of playing his advisers against each other. The power wielded by the staff officer – a strong believer in centralization – is originally based upon his special knowledge but rests immediately upon the chief executive's opinion of him. He is powerful in that he stands at the chief's elbow. He is powerless from the moment the chief turns against him, asking the advice of someone else. As compared with the line manager his position rests only upon opinion. The greater his knowledge, moreover, the less he may be able to see the picture as a whole. Should he be too strong a personality there is a danger that the balance of direction may be upset, and the company produce what it cannot sell, or advertise what it cannot supply, with its personnel happy but its account overdrawn. There is always a danger in allowing a specialist to become chief executive.

Line management is represented by the barons or plant managers, by the heads of divisions and the chief executives of subsidiary companies. These may have their own specialist advisers on whom they rely in turn. The baron, earl or marquis (in feudal terms) lacks the advantage of standing at the king's elbow. His territory may be remote and his visits to head office infrequent, but in contrast to the departmental chiefs on the staff side, he stands on his own feet and rules his own territory. He bases his power, moreover, upon his own measurable success, the profit derived from the capital investment in his division of plant. His strength is a matter of fact and not merely of opinion. He is unlikely to be replaced as long as he delivers the goods. And if his success compares well with the other plant managers he stands in line to succeed the chief executive, since he has general skills and his efficiency has been proved. He stands in the direct line of authority, receiving orders from above and issuing more detailed orders to those below him in the organization. He may wish at times that there were less interference from head office, because he does better when left on his own. The daydream may include the idea of his division becoming an independent company – which can actually happen – and he may wish at times that line, as opposed to staff, management were more strongly represented at head office. Conceding the need for a general policy he tends to be a strong advocate for decentralization.

The company's organization is a great deal more complex than this, however. First, line management will be represented at head office, perhaps in the person of the deputy chief and often in the persons of other directors. Second, the chain of command from the chief executive to the divisional head to the plant manager is apt to be paralleled by the departmental channel of communication, as from one accountant to another or from the senior research man to one lower in the hierarchy. Companies differ from each other in their lines of communication, partly because their directors have different ideas and partly because they are not all in the same line of business. It is also worth bearing in mind that the differing attitudes of the chief accountant and the plant manager may reflect their present positions rather than their respective personalities. Let the plant manager move to head office and he will soon see the need for a consistent policy throughout the group and a standardized procedure under central control. Move the chief accountant to the plant manager's former position and he will probably see that decentralization is needed in order to encourage initiative among those who do the actual work. There is no end to this particular argument, but we need to realize that modern technology has made centralized control at least technically possible. The effect successively of the steamship and railway, the telegraph and telephone, the typewriter and duplicating machine, the car and the aircraft, the telex and the computer, has been to put head office in close touch with every part of the organization. It is arguable that interference is encouraged by the fact that the means to interfere exist, and that what is now possible is not necessarily wise. But much depends on the current situation and the golden rule, if there is one, is still to be found.

The central difficulty in the direction of big business is one of proportion and balance. There must be a balance of power between the specialists and the generalists, between the various specialists themselves and the board. It is when the balance is upset that disaster looms. Where the finance men have too much power the company may fall behind in terms of research and development. When the engineers gain control the product may be superb but priced out of the market. Where head office does too much the group will produce statistics instead of goods. When it does too little, the divisions may go bankrupt. This last danger was illustrated in the case of General Dynamics, which lost in 1960–2, the sum of $425 million, perhaps the biggest loss that any company has ever sustained. General Dynamics has since been reorganized but took the form of a loose federation with nine divisions and 106,000 people on the payroll. Each of the divisions had been an independent corporation and each was still organized as such, complete with its president and staff. The Convair division was the most important, with aircraft factories at Fort Worth, Pomona and San Diego. This sprawling empire was theoretically controlled by a New York central office with a thirty-two-man board mainly composed of financiers and lawyers and an office staff of about two hundred. The trouble began when Convair accepted from TWA the task of producing a medium-range jet aircraft. The programme was agreed by the executive committee and Convair began to design and build the 880, which was presently upgraded as the 990. Priced at $4,700,000 (before anyone knew what it would cost) it would break even as a venture, it was thought, when two hundred had been sold. The actual firm orders for the 990 numbered twenty-three and General Dynamics, by 1963, had a debt of $350 million. This disaster was entirely due to optimistic planning by Convair, combined with so large a measure of decentralization that the General Dynamics board had possessed neither information nor the means of control.

The fact that decentralization can mean disaster is no proof that the opposite is any recipe for success. It was the strong and centralized control of the Ford Motor Company which made the Ford so successful in the early days of mass production. It was the same strong and centralized control which kept the one model in production for too long and prepared the way for General Motors' still greater success with a wider range of better cars. It was, in fact, the federal structure of General Motors which allowed it to attack so successfully on such a broad front. A more recent disaster can be traced to a different cause,

the search for technical perfection at the expense of commercial survival. There can be little doubt that the Rolls Royce failure in 1971 was due to the engineers being supreme (as might seem natural) in an engineering business. Rolls Royce made its name on a luxury car but its actual business (or ninety-five per cent of it) rested upon the design and construction of aircraft engines. As each aircraft is essentially built around an engine, there is no more vital business than engine design. This rests, however, on experiment and the early stages of development will include failures, a dozen ideas being tried and only one accepted. In estimating the probable cost, the difficulty is to guess how many failures there will be and how far they will go before they are cancelled. Rolls Royce was technically

Lockheed's noble side: they become the first US firm to adopt a Plan for Progress, when their president signs a pledge aimed at achieving equal employment opportunities, in the presence of President Kennedy, LBJ and Labour Secretary Arthur Goldberg in the White House . . .

successful with its engines, nevertheless, failing only to break into the big US market, dominated by Pratt and Whitney and General Electric. In 1961 Rolls Royce's chief executive, Sir Denning Pearson, changed the company's accounting methods and produced the Spey engine, which sold fairly well – outside the USA. In order to break into the US market he allowed David Huddie, his engineer salesman, to offer Lockheed a new type of jet engine for the L-1011, otherwise known as the Tri-Star airbus. To secure the order, Huddie (who was knighted for it) fixed a low price of $840,000 for each RB 211 engine and promised delivery in 1971 at a development cost of $156 million. The contract was signed in April 1968 and work began on an engine which was to use untested material and untried design so as to be nearly twice as powerful as anything in actual use.

Technical problems multiplied and were tackled resolutely by a group of technical perfectionists. The original estimate of $156 million for development costs became $180 million, then $324 million and so rose to 'at least' $408 million. It now became apparent that each engine, already sold for $840,000, would cost 1,104,000 to make. There would also be colossal penalties payable because of late delivery – $120 million

... and its less noble side: Rolls Royce crashes.

Lockheed's chairman,
Daniel J. Haughton in
London during the Rolls
Royce crisis. Haughton
was Lockheed's sole
representative.

or more. Rolls Royce had already had some government help and now asked for more. It then became apparent that any further help would be a drop in the ocean. The company was bankrupt, killed by a combination of technical excellence and optimistic finance. In the Tri-Star, Lockheed possessed, as someone said 'the largest glider in the world'. Of the three hundred and fifty aircraft that Lockheed needed to sell merely to break even, only a hundred and seventy-eight had been sold by August 1970. To make matters worse, the Lockheed Aircraft Corporation was itself in financial difficulties, having lost heavily on a military contract and been smitten at Burbank by, of all things, an earthquake. From the point of view of corporate structure two interesting facts emerge. In the first place the financial and accounting experts on the Rolls Royce board seem to have had little influence and still less knowledge of what was happening. Pearson and Huddie were dedicated engineers, intent on producing the world's best aero-engine. To their aid came Frederick Corfield, Minister of Aviation Supply, intent on saving British prestige. There was little thought for the shareholders. The second interesting fact is that the Lockheed Aircraft Corporation was not represented in negotiation by its executive committee, still less by its board, but solely by its former president and current chairman, Daniel Jeremiah Haughton, described as 'one of the last of the great corporate autocrats'. A systems analyst by trade, Haughton has been with Lockheed since 1933. He did not become president by any very democratic process, being the nominee of the syndicate which saved Lockheed from going bankrupt on an earlier occasion.

Some authors make much of the extent to which big business is really controlled by the institutional investors: the banks, the insurance companies and unit trusts. Richard J. Barber, for example, points out that the US banks administer a capital sum of six hundred billion dollars:

... Just forty-nine banks, of the size and notoriety of Morgan Guaranty, Chase Manhattan, Bank of America, and First National City, hold more than half of the country's total bank trust assets. With this immense sum at their disposal, backed up by their position as primary lenders of capital, these bank colossi have acquired trustee ownership of enough common stock ... to provide effective control of about 150 of the five hundred largest US industrial corporations. To ensconce this massive position further, these forty-nine banks have placed their representatives on the boards of the directors of three hundred of the nation's biggest companies.[6]

He goes on to emphasize that just one of the commercial banks, the Morgan Guaranty, has assets of seventeen billion dollars and holds five per cent or more of the equity in seventy-two corporations. That sort of percentage, backed by a single director, is something short of control, as he admits, but 'the whisper of a giant . . . is . . . more likely to be heeded than the shout of a midget'. This we may readily believe, and we are left with the picture of each president or managing director as a mere puppet in the hands of a commercial bank representative. If we accept the accuracy of this picture at all we may think it most nearly true in Germany where the banks are thought to be very influential indeed. Elsewhere this picture fails to convince. It is true that the bank representative is there, but does he wield the power he might in theory possess? We are not to know what happens in the boardroom, still less what is said over the telephone before the board even meets, but evidence for the banker's decisive influence seems to be conspicuously absent. His main purpose, one might guess, should be to protect the value of the bank's investment. His voice should be heard uttering counsels of restraint and caution. If he is really so influential, and if that is the direction in which his influence is exerted, why is his advice ignored? We are brought back, in fact, to the example of General Dynamics in 1960–2. The executive committee which approved the decision to go ahead with the 880, included the president, a banker, two investment bankers, two oilmen and five lawyers. The technicians, eager to make a sensational breakthrough, were actually outnumbered by the bankers and lawyers who should have opposed gambling with the stockholders' money. Nor is the Rolls Royce story completely different. There was responsible advice in plenty but the company went bankrupt. The fact would seem to be that the big corporation is governed by its executive officers and exists for itself. Kenneth Galbraith has invented the word 'techno-structure' to describe the group which is actually responsible for corporation policy: 'It embraces all who bring specialized knowledge, talent or experience to group decision-making. This, not the management, is the guiding intelligence – the brain – of the enterprise.' This may be as near to the truth as we are likely to come, but is it really possible to generalize? Corporations differ in their purpose and are not all organized in the same way. Whether technocrats or financiers have the last word may well depend upon the nature of the business. But the trend is probably away from the financier, if only because the problems have become so complex and obscure. It is easier to approve than reject a proposal wrapped in terms which are, to the layman, practically meaningless. Some recent decisions, both governmental and industrial, can hardly be explained in any other way. If it is difficult to explain decisions such as those leading to the Rolls Royce fiasco, it is even more difficult to spot who actually took them. This compels us to consider the role of the committee.

The basic concept of comitology, as this subject is called, is that the committee, in its original and primitive form, will normally comprise five members. In the world of government the four members were

OPPOSITE
'I never did feel happy about Rolls Royce – they were too damn quiet for my liking.' A cartoonist's comment on the White House summing-up of the Rolls Royce–Lockheed fiasco.

versed, respectively, in finance, foreign policy, defence and law; the
fifth, who has failed to master any of these subjects, is thus inevitably
in the chair. In the world of commerce and industry the four members
were similarly versed in finance, production, marketing and law and the
fifth, without special knowledge, is the chairman. Five is the ideal
number for competence, secrecy and speed but there are forces at
work which tend to increase the number of members. Others come
to be included, some because they have special expertise, some because
they represent interests which demand representation, and others
again because they add prestige or because their exclusion would be
dangerous. On a board of directors the additional executives might
be experts in advertising and personnel management, the others
representing the stockholders (both great and small) or else generally
lending distinction or neutralizing external attack. By the time the
members have thus risen to twenty or more the original five have
formed the habit of meeting on the previous day and settling everything in what comes to be called the executive committee. When that
in turn becomes too big an inner group will form again with some other
title and so *ad infinitum*. Whatever its size or composition, this inner
group will be dominated by the company's key figure, the chief
executive, though his exact title is a cause of some confusion. In US
practice the chief executive is the president, the chairman of the board
being an elder statesman whose importance becomes crucial only when
a new president has to be appointed. In Britain the structure is roughly
the same but the president is called the managing director. In both
countries it is possible, though unusual, for the same man to be both
chairman and managing director. In Germany and the Netherlands,
the president is usually what Americans would call the chairman,
the chief executive being the general manager. There are considerable variations both in terminology and practice but most corporations
and companies have an active chief who runs the business. The theory
of business organization is that major decisions are taken by the board
of directors, possibly on the advice of a committee, and that effect
is given to each decision by the president whose instructions are
given to the departmental heads concerned. What actually happens
may be different, or at least more complex, but we should at least keep
this theory in mind.

Before the First World War the big company usually had a departmental organization. A chain store enterprise, for example, would
have departments dealing respectively with finance, purchasing and

A *Punch* cartoonist's view of the boardroom.

personnel, with sales and advertising; to which might be added, in course of time, departments in charge of real estate, testing and research. Apart from these service departments there would be district managers and store managers. Even large industrial firms, dealing mostly with a single product, had as simple an organization as this. When this sort of structure began to break down, it was partly because of growing size but still more because of diversification. It was being found that substances like rubber and oil could be transformed into all sorts of consumer goods. Chemical by-products multiplied, leading the manufacturers into markets they had not even considered. Trade outlets expanded, leading in different directions, and the resulting complex of interests became more and more difficult to administer. Old captains of industry resisted any major reorganization, sometimes killing themselves with overwork, but their successors, some with military experience in the First World War, saw that the time had come to decentralize. The most important man to reach this conclusion was Pierre du Pont who reorganized the chemical firm of EI du Pont de Nemours in 1920. Pierre du Pont's innovations were three: the executive committee, the finance committee and the product division. He had perceived, first of all, that the board of directors had become too large. With its full-time professional members he formed the executive committee. With its treasurer and outside finance men he formed the finance committee. As from then, the full board met only seldom and ceremonially. The factories were then organized in five groups, each based not on its locality but on what it produced, whether explosives or fertilizers. The groups were made largely autonomous from that point, the service departments (advertising, sales, etc.) being reproduced at the group headquarters. Each group had its own balance sheet and each traded to make a profit. Pressure on head office was reduced and line management was strengthened by inter-group rivalry.

Pierre du Pont had hardly reorganized EI du Pont de Nemours before he was made president of General Motors (1921), a firm which he reorganized in exactly the same way, the vehicles being grouped according to price range. Other major concerns watched the results of decentralization but were slow to follow suit. Westinghouse and Sears Roebuck decentralized in 1929 but further imitation seems to have been delayed by the slump and by the Second World War. There may have been some military influence, for reorganization then followed in a big way. International Harvester decentralized in 1943,

Allied Chemicals in 1945, General Electric and the Ford Motor Company in 1946 and Chrysler in 1950. A wave of reorganization followed throughout the world, the fashion being to form four or five groups each sometimes comprising several divisions. The executive committee would then comprise the president and his assistant, the vice-president of each group and the vice-presidents heading some or all of the service departments at head office, these departments usually numbering nine or ten. Once actual power was thus centred in the executive committee of twelve or fourteen, the number of directors on the board itself could happily expand to thirty or more. Its relationship to the executive committee was now very much that of the British Privy Council to the Cabinet and we might fairly ask at this point what function the board still retained other than that of appointing the president. One useful action it could carry out was giving the title of 'director' (like the Privy Councillor's 'Right Honourable') which could now be widely conferred as a compliment or consolation prize – as a reward for long, if undistinguished service.

But the neatest organization can break down in the face of the determination of one chief executive. Such is the case of Harold Geneen and his ITT. The International Telephone and Telegraph Corporation is a financial conglomerate, and this fact is fairly reflected in its top-level organization. In 1972 there were eighteen directors on the board, of which seven were company executives. The seven comprised Harold S. Geneen (chairman and president since 1959), three executive vice-presidents and three senior vice-presidents. There was then an executive committee with nine members, headed again by Mr Geneen but excluding the other company executives. The committee members were:

Eugene R. Black – Consultant.
George R. Brown – Oil and investments.
Alvin E. Friedman – Kuhn, Loeb and Co.
Arthur M. Hill – Investments.
J. Patrick Lauren – Financial Consultant.
John A. McCone – Chairman, Hendy International (Shipping).
Warren L. Pearson – Chairman, All America Cable & Radio.
Felix G. Rohatyn – Lazard Freres & Co.

Two merchants banks were thus represented, both Kuhn, Loeb & Co. and Lazard Freres. It is worthy of note that Lazard Freres

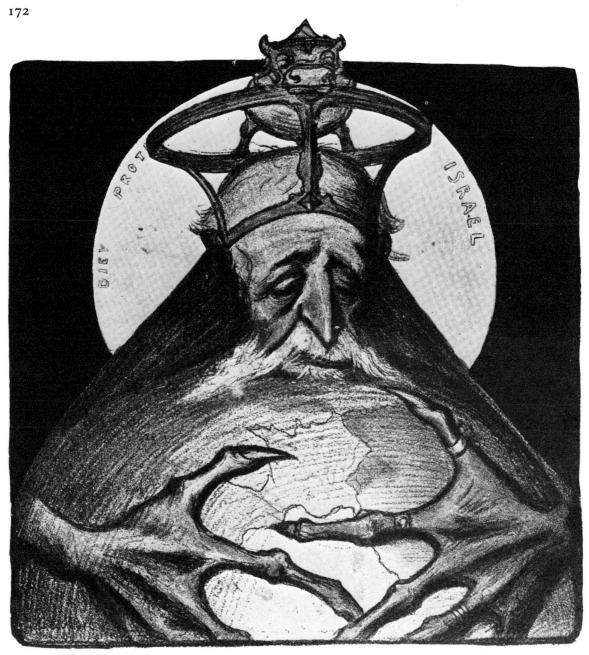

A vision of the happy face of capitalism embracing the world, entitled 'Optimism'.

have been called 'the merger bank' from having played a vital part in such deals as those in which RCA took over Random House and Hertz, the McDonnell Corporation took over the Douglas Aircraft Company, Loew's Theatres took over Lorillard and Kinney National Services took over Warner Brothers. So the presence of Rohatyn and

Friedman was of much more than ceremonial importance. With them sat four other investment experts and Mr Pearson, chairman of an ITT subsidiary, the corporation staff being represented only by the chairman and president. The ITT executive committee was rather similar in composition to what another corporation would call the finance committee; a frank admission that ITT is largely a financial concern. Alongside the executive committee was the management policy committee numbering eighteen. Headed by the chairman and president, this comprised the six 'inside' directors who were not on the executive committee, an executive vice-president who is not a director, three senior vice-presidents, one senior vice-president and general-counsel, one senior vice-president and comptroller and one vice-president and treasurer. Of the two committees the one consisted entirely of corporation officers, the other almost entirely of outside consultants. Beneath this level the management of innumerable divisions was entrusted to thirty-seven vice-presidents with responsi-bilities which ranged from flight simulators to radar, from Apollo 12 to equipment for Concorde. Other and more recently formed conglomerates have only small head office staffs under boards with the same bias as ITT, and regard this pattern as conducive to economy in overheads.

ITT began, as its name suggests, as a firm manufacturing telegraphic and telephone equipment. To move from there into other electrical work was a normal development but Harold Geneen had induced ITT to acquire the Sheraton Hotel Group, the Avis car-hire firm, Continental Bakeries, the Hartford Insurance Company (bought for $1.5 billion,) Abbey Life Insurance, Shirley dog food and Amplex. He also invaded Europe on so large a scale that ITT's European subsidiaries employ 200,000 people and 36,000 in Britain alone. Our immediate concern is not with these foreign conquests nor with the scandal that surrounded ITT in 1971 but with the way in which such a corporation is organized. In shaping its investment policy a significant part was played by Mr Rohatyn, the director who represents Lazard Freres. The acquisitions were financed by, and some of them suggested by, the merchant bankers. It is not apparent that the bankers have much say in ITT apart from that. We have seen its official structure but the truth is that ITT is run by Mr Geneen, whose salary (fixed at $812,000) is the highest paid to anyone in the USA and this fact makes it easier to understand how the business is run. If all the vice-presidents were working independently, the one man at the summit might at least have time to breathe. But the I T T empire is in fact highly centralized, which makes Geneen's system the more remarkable. It was brilliantly described by Anthony Sampson,[7] who emphasized that Geneen is, above all, a super-accountant, and one whose interests are solely in statistical information. The strain on his immediate lieutenants, six of them paid over $200,000 a year, would seem to be considerable:

> But it is in Europe that Geneen's system of control is most dramatic, for here it takes the physical form of a monthly invasion. On the last Monday of every month, a Boeing 727 takes off from New York to Brussels, with sixty ITT executives aboard – often including Geneen himself, with a special office rigged up for him to work in. For four days they stay in Brussels, still insulated in their special ITT world: many of them keep their watches on New York time. Most of their time is spent in the marathon meetings which are the core of the system.
>
> A meeting is a weird spectacle, with more than a hint (as one of them complained) of Dr Strangelove. About 120 people are assembled in the specially equipped fourth-floor room, with cool air-conditioning, soft lighting and discreet microphones. The curtains are drawn against the daylight and a big screen displays endless tables of statistics. Round a big horse-shoe table sit the top men of ITT from America and Europe, like diplomats at a conference. In the middle, swivelling and rocking to and fro in his armchair, surveying the faces and gazing at the statistics, is an owlish figure behind a label saying HAROLD S. GENEEN.

The strength of this system lies partly in Geneen's obsession with his corporation, for he has no other interests of any kind, partly in his genius for figures and partly (it is claimed) because he and his top executives have no sentimental involvement with any of the products they offer, whether dog food or face cream. They want to see a high return on capital and will dispose at once of any subsidiary that does not pay – or any executive, for that matter, who fails to show a profit from his division. Some US politicians are concerned about ITT's monopolistic tendencies and others are still more alarmed about the pressure which ITT can exert in Washington or indeed upon the political situation in Chile, but what is probably more important is the example ITT offers of a centralized organization run on a system of sophisticated accountancy. There may be a general pattern of decentralization but there are exceptions to the rule and ITT is the supreme example.

Not every corporation is a conglomerate and not every president will give himself completely to one single and complex task. It has come to be thought indeed that some tasks of leadership are beyond the powers of any one man. It was apparently in this belief that the twenty-three directors of General Motors decided to establish a system of shared responsibility in 1971. As chairman of their twenty-four-billion-dollar-a-year corporation they elected Richard C. Gerstenberg, previously vice-chairman and a specialist in finance. As president they retained Edward Cole, engineer and salesman, who is also to be chairman of the executive committee. As vice-chairman they appointed Thomas A. Murphy, another finance man with manufacturing experience. The tradition in the USA has been to give the title of vice-chairman as consolation prize to someone who is given little responsibility. This pattern is changing and the vice-chairmanship is now regarded in some firms as a step towards the summit. At Avon Products there is even a vice-chairman who is also chief executive. Westinghouse and Gillette both have two vice-chairmen, executive, and with heavy responsibilities. Said *Business Week* on this subject, in December 1971:

In recent years, the concept of collective top management for multi-billion dollar and multinational corporations has become commonplace in industry. Some fifty major corporations, including Gulf Oil Corp and General Electric Co have opted for an office of the president or a similar group structure at the top.

The idea of sharing responsibility at the corporation summit derives from the fact that some new factors have now to be considered other than those of production, marketing and finance. The major industrial corporation is today more involved with government, with the universities and with other countries than previously. On the political side the industrial giant is concerned, on the one hand, with defence contracts, on the other hand with the anti-pollution lobby. A corporation like General Electric or ITT can hardly afford to refuse government contracts, which can be highly profitable in themselves and still more profitable in their indirect results. The ideal is to have government pay for the development costs of an aircraft which can then be modified for commercial use. The same spin-off benefits can be obtained on a smaller scale from all sorts of smaller machines and instruments, including those ordered and subsequently cancelled. The possibilities are obvious and so, unfortunately, are the risks. For governments come and go, yesterday's policy being dead today and possibly due for revival tomorrow. To succeed in this uncertain and possibly corrupt world the industrialist needs to have a thorough knowledge of the political scene; a greater knowledge than a dedicated engineer is likely to have or can probably acquire. The anti-pollution and road-safety lobbies add a fresh complication to the scene, compelling the industrialist to foresee (as well as he can) the pressures to which government will be subject and the reactions to which each pressure will give rise. There was once an idea that the wise industrialist should be able to foresee the economic trend. This is less important, as we now realize, than to foresee the fashion in economic theory. To have read the textbook is not as profitable as to have listened at the keyhole.

There is also a new relationship between industry and higher education. Mention of the word 'university' makes many people think today of bearded weirdies, student processions, ill-qualified and anarchist lecturers and useless people generally of repulsive appearance. People tend to forget that the university may also include research laboratories and some hundreds of inconspicuous but hard-working technologists, whose work may be very significant indeed. The more important of these tend to be associated with both government and industry, their research projects being financed from outside the university. This is a two-way process, the industrialists supplying the university with funds for specific programmes, the university supplying the industrialists with talent and advice. It is symbolized by some recent appointments in General Motors, Ernest Starkman as vice-president for environmental affairs, Paul F. Chenea as vice-president for research and Stephen H. Fuller as vice-president for personnel administration. Starkman was professor of engineering at the University of California, Chenea a science professor at Purdue and Fuller a professor at the Harvard School of Business Administration. In the same way David Lewis, formerly of General Motors, is now a professor at the University of Michigan. The dividing line between government, business and university is no longer very firmly drawn.

There is, finally, the international side of business. In our discussion earlier, it became apparent that big business must always cross national frontiers and become multinational in character. This must create the need for the industrial diplomatist, the man who can reconcile economic interests with nationalistic sentiments. The more backward countries of the world, often blessed with valuable resources, cheap labour and potential markets, are usually eager for industrial development and yet hostile towards foreign management. It is the task of the industrial diplomatist to master the complexities of tribal politics and provide a management which is in fact alien but which looks indigenous, and also a relationship with government which looks subordinate but is actually dominant. These are not the sort of tasks which can be entrusted to a systems analyst or production engineer. Men are needed with a broader experience and a different outlook, just such men as the oil companies have been able to recruit and deploy in the Middle East. This need for diplomacy adds another dimension to big business and a further justification for dividing the responsibilities of top management between men of diverse gifts. No one man can do, or even understand, all that has to be done.

We have seen that, while there are fashions and trends in the possible patterns of management, there is still every variety in existence. There are some firms that are run by their founder as president or chairman, some by the founder's family and others managed by professional directors but still in family ownership. Nor do such companies tend to disappear, for new industries are still founded, starting the sequence all over again. The majority of big firms are publicly owned however, and managed for the shareholder (so the textbook explains) by an elected board of directors. The directors are in fact appointed by themselves and by each other, sometimes from within the company and sometimes from other institutions concerned with finance. The number of directors may be great or small. Where it is under eighteen they may have retained effective control. Where their number is over twenty they will usually be found to have lost their power to an executive committee, reserving little more than their right to appoint the chief executive. But the executive committee in its turn may lose its power to the chairman or president – still more to the man who is both – provided only that he is sufficiently dominant and the firm under his rule is sufficiently successful. Big business today affords examples of every form of organization; rule by one man, by a select few, or by many.

5 OF GOVERNMENT AND UNIONS

Big business has its philanthropists, but philanthropy is not its main goal. Bigger profits and more growth – in short, bigger business – are the main aims of the major companies and also the little ones. These are not necessarily the chief prerequisites of those who work on the shop floor, nor of governments who, whether capitalist or socialist, need popularity and votes. Hence business is in something of a state of perpetual warfare with the power of organized labour and often with governments which have, in various countries, passed legislation to deal with the abuses of monopoly, price-fixing and redundancy.

Industrial dispute is as old as industry. In England, for example, a combination of workmen was from early times an illegal conspiracy. For our present purposes, however, we need not go back to medieval origins. Mass labour movements began, in effect, with mass production and that, like big business itself, began with the US railways. Railway tracks and rifles were among the first things to be manufactured on a large scale and there could be no major, widespread unrest until there was major industry. Yet the industrial revolution began in Britain, and so did the trade union in its modern form. Our opening date is 1824, the year in which Francis Place and Joseph Hume managed to secure the repeal of the Combination acts of 1799 and 1800. More or less legalized, the trade unions came into the open, the most militant among them being that of the miners. At a time when the French Revolution was still a recent memory there were many who feared a mass movement of the poor. However, trade union activity was usually confined to the more prosperous workmen in the more highly skilled trades. Moreover, this had always been so, the earliest unions (often described as Friendly Societies) being formed among compositors, hatters, coopers, sailmakers, shoemakers and shipwrights. After 1824 some of the local unions came together on a national or at least regional scale. These groups included the Northumberland and Durham Colliers' Union, the Cotton Spinners' Union (Lancashire), the Potters' Union (Staffordshire) and the

The Amalgamated Society
of Engineers was founded
in 1851.

BE UNITED AND INDUSTRIOUS

AMALGAMATED SOCIETY OF ENGINEERS, MACHINISTS, MILLWRIGHTS,
SMITHS, AND PATTERN MAKERS.

Another early trade union
card.

Clothiers' Union (Yorkshire). The more genuinely national organizations included those of the Carpenters and Joiners and, more significantly, the Steam Engine Makers, formed in 1824. This last group was the early nineteenth-century equivalent of a union formed today among technicians concerned with nuclear fission. They must have been the very élite of the working class, the forerunners of the men who formed the Amalgamated Society of Engineers in 1851.

For purposes of comparison it is worth remarking that the middle-class unions date from much the same period, the Institution of Civil Engineers from 1818, the Law Society from 1825 and the British Medical Association from 1832. The concern of the skilled workmen was with wages and the middle class with status, but neither group could be regarded as revolutionary. Nor was it easy to reach agreement among trade unionists who were so sharply distinguished from each other in their standards of living. The first concern of the skilled workman is always to preserve a wage differential between himself and the man whose skill is less. So the attempt to form a Grand National Consolidated Trades Union (1833) was not a success, and the United Kingdom Alliance of Organized Trades (1866) was as shortlived. What was more successful was the spread of socialist doctrine, partly through the influence of Robert Owen and similar idealists and partly through the process by which workmen took to reading the books and pamphlets published by such men as John Cassell from about the middle of the century. Much thought went into union organization and all the later unions had constitutions based upon that of the Amalgamated Society of Engineers. The movement was strong in London but stronger still in the counties north of the Humber and Dee where there were 726,000 union members by 1892. Total membership came to a million and a half by that period, comprising about twenty per cent of the wage-earning populace. By then the movement had begun to spread to the less highly skilled and less highly paid groups of wage-earners. This trend was symbolized by the dock strike of 1889 and the formation of unions among the gasworkers and railwaymen. By the end of the century the British labour movement was well established, the trade unions (for workers) being paralleled by the co-operative societies (for consumers). Twentieth-century 'progress' was well defined before the century had even begun. It came to be embodied in the programme of the Labour Party as outlined by Sidney Webb in 1894.

The industrial revolution came later to the other European

Yes Gentlemen, these is my principles, — no K—g, — no L—ds, — no Parsons, — no Police, — no Taxes.

A meeting of the trade unions in 1834. Contemporary ridicule of the trade union movement.

countries with the result, in many instances, that socialist parties were established before the trade unions had been organized at the national level. This was true for example, in Germany, Austria, Sweden, Norway, Denmark and Belgium. The Germans thus had their Social Democratic Party in 1870, and their National Executive Commission for the union movement in 1890. For this reason these countries have had a more doctrinaire type of socialism, springing from the activities of middle-class intellectuals whose views are more extreme than those of trade union officials. Following the process by which unions have been absorbed into a political party the membership has become predominantly artisan, but is still less practical and more likely to arouse opposition than the British Labour Party. Sweden is usually regarded as the prime example of success achieved by a Social Democratic Party with union support. Success in this context is partially due, some say, to the fact that Swedish society was egalitarian in structure before the socialist gospel was preached.

'BREAKERS AHEAD'
A *Punch* cartoon of the
1880s showing John Bull
saying '*For goodness' sake,
do try to pull together.*'

France differs from every other country in this respect, having never recovered from the revolution which tore its society apart. French workmen have had the vote since 1848 but they have often been hostile towards government, so much so that their unions affirmed their hatred of politics in 1906. The situation was further confused by clerical and anti-clerical attitudes, with the result that many of the trade unions came under communist or anarchist influence while others, under church patronage, were distinguished as 'Christian' and are now labelled as 'democratic'. The industrial revolution came late to France. The family firm long predominated in French industry and there was little mass production before about 1930. When mass strikes occurred during the political ferment of 1936 it transpired that the unions were more regional than national. For those not actually resident in France the French pattern of politics and trade unionism is extremely difficult to understand.

US trade unions were confined at first to skilled workers in certain industries. In a land of republican institutions and supposedly equal opportunity, with the open frontier and great mobility of population, there was no great tradition of social protest. Nor did the US trade unionists agree with the process (as in England) by which trade unions came to be absorbed by a political party.

The process of spreading unionism to the semi-skilled and unskilled workers was long delayed in the United States. It occurred only in the wake of the great social upheaval of the 1930s when unionism was finally extended to the mass-production industries. Partially as a consequence of this long delay, the leaders of the American unions of skilled workers created for themselves a special union ideology that 'gloried' in its practicality and its pragmatism. The unions had no ideological approach to the economy and society as a whole. . . .[1]

Whereas the European trade unionists were intent on reforming the whole of society, and replacing ancient privilege by democratic equality, the US unions accepted society as it was and put all their effort into gaining specific and immediate advantages for themselves. As time went on, they used their voting strength to promote legislation or influence particular candidates for office, but results came slowly in terms of welfare on the national scale. The consequence was that fringe benefits including pension rights and medical aid remained within the sphere of union rather than political activity. As a further consequence the aim of the US trade unionist has always been to reach a written collective agreement with the employer. The emphasis, moreover, has been on an agreement reached between a single employer and a single union, or at most between the union and a group of employers in the same area. The mere size of the USA was enough, at first, to discourage negotiation on a wider scale. Since then it has been apparent that the big and prosperous company can be persuaded to make more generous concessions than could be extracted from the industry as a whole or from the committee of an employers' association.

National differences apart, a trade union must fall into one of four basic categories. In its earliest and most primitive form the union may be formed among the workmen at a given factory or mine. It can then extend to those of the same trade throughout a district. The final stage (which may or may not be reached) is to form a national union in a given industry. It would be theoretically possible to form an international union, but attempts in this direction have achieved little success. Considering these alternatives, we come to realize

that the technological trend favours the union which covers a trade rather than an industry. Given a relatively simple process of manufacture, as in an early sawmill or windmill, all those employed could be described as sawyers or millers; masters, journeymen or apprentices in the same trade. Given a more technically advanced factory the staff will include engineers, electricians, boilermen, truck drivers and storemen. These will bring with them a differing background and a complex pecking order, with wage differentials based upon conditions of apprenticeship and scarcity of talent. And whereas it is possible to have a national union of all railwaymen, the more probable pattern is one which provides a separate union for maintenance staff, for telegraphists, for booking clerks and for railway police. Different groups have distinct and even opposing interests and the final situation is one in which a whole industry can be paralysed by a strike organized within a single small but essential group of specialists.

What is the relationship between trade unions and big business? Would it be true to say that the big firm creates the big union? Certainly, there is some reason to think so. Workers may feel that they have to deal with a large and expert organization, one with vast financial resources and controlled by men they have scarcely seen and might not even recognize. To contend with such a faceless monster they feel the need for as large an organization on their side, one with its own reserve funds and legal advisers. There is, as we shall see, a sense in which the trade union thus models itself on its opponent. As against that, the big union does not, as a rule, correspond in its membership to that of the industrial group to which its wage claim is addressed. There are few instances of a strike organized by all the employees of a given industrial concern, save perhaps where the industry has been nationalized. The strike will more commonly originate in a single trade and will sometimes be caused by internal disagreement between one trade and another. For minimizing industrial dispute the ideal plan would be one which allowed each management to negotiate with a single union. That is not, however, the situation which exists and our picture of big business would be incomplete if it were not accompanied by a reminder that the unions can be just as big and as well organized as business itself. Where the unions differ most sharply from big business is in the fact that union members are more vocal than shareholders, with the result that while directors can decide, union officials can only advise.

Faced by big business, the workers of the world have very often united in big unions and these, like other organizations, have tended to copy their opponents' style and method. A good example of this in Britain is the Transport and General Workers' Union. This conglomerate was formed by Ernest Bevin in 1922 from fourteen previously separate unions. It bears the stamp of his personality in that its general secretary is elected by ballot and is supported by a council of part-time members, all appointed by him. This concentration of power can be justified by the fact that the interests of the union

Ernest Bevin, one of the great figures in trade-union history, who formed the huge Transport and General Workers Union.

are otherwise highly dispersed. Its militant core is provided by the dock workers but it also comprises bus drivers, truck drivers, vehicle maintenance men and a number of vaguely related and unrelated groups. Its membership is enormous – some one and a half million – and its funds considerable. It was the first British union to build itself a permanent headquarters in London, in Transport House, 1928. It is an office block on eight floors 'within a stone's throw of the House of Lords', of which a part has been let to the Labour Party. Far from throwing stones at the House of Lords, the union officials have been more ready to take their seats in it. The big union soon looks like any other big organization, complex, expensive, cumbersome and forbidding. To the more nervous applicant it looks as formidable as the head office of the firm which has so heartlessly discharged him. More coherent in structure, and once as important in the movement, was the National Union of Miners with funds at one time of £170 million and investments which included the freehold of the Café Royal. So massive are these organizations, that they are themselves employers, and mean enough in that capacity to have had industrial unrest among their own office staff.

Tradition and customary procedure limits the trade union to a limited function of demanding higher wages and improved fringe benefits in return for less work done in fewer hours. They have seldom revealed any interest in the efficiency of the firm or the quality of the work. They rarely demand a voice in the management. Theirs is a mainly negative function and the leaders' fear is that working with the management will lose them the confidence of the rank and file. To be re-elected the union officers have to be aggressive. Each year they must frame a new demand and one that is at least equal in value to the amount of the subscription. Members expect to see some return for their money and where no grievance exists it will have to be invented. Failing some action on the part of its officials a union will begin to lose membership, often to another union. This is made possible by the extent to which functions may overlap in the more technologically advanced industries.

Contributing to nearly constant industrial unrest at the great Ford plant in Dagenham, England, which employs around fifty-eight thousand workers, is the presence there of more than twenty unions – a number of which have overlapping jurisdictions. One British union official, from a union *not* involved at Dagenham, has argued: 'The existence of twenty-two

OPPOSITE Government *v.* Unions: a picture taken at the height of trade-union opposition to the Industrial Relations Bill.

separate unions in one factory makes it impossible for satisfactory negotiations to be maintained.'

Industrial relations in the British motor car industry were back in the news again in 1966 with the report of the special Motor Industry Joint Labour Council, which found that there were six hundred stoppages in eight car firms in the first six months of the year, all but five unofficial.

The situation in the motor car industry is, of course, the worst in Britain, but it does point up what has been a vexing and fairly widespread problem in British trade union life, especially in the engineering industries. [The relatively rapid rate of technological change] . . . aggravates labour problems in that sector as jobs must constantly be redefined and wage incentive rates changed.[2]

If British and European trade unions are unwieldy in organization they are nothing compared with the larger unions formed in the USA. There were strikes in the USA from the early days of the industrial revolution and numerous attempts to form trade unions. It is broadly true to say that the really big unions were first established as a result of New Deal legislation in the 1930s. One of the most important was, and is, the United Steelworkers of America, centred on Pittsburgh. This gained the recognition of US Steel in 1937, its members gaining a forty-hour week (it had been an eighty-four-hour week in 1900). Recognition by Republic Mills and the Bethlehem Steel Company followed the famous 'Chicago Massacre' and the union has since been conspicuously well organized. Its strike of 1946 affected 1,292 companies in thirty states. The steelworkers then became the hard core of a wider movement, the Committee for Industrial Organization (CIO) with its subsidiary Political Action Committee. Within this wide group came such militant unions as the National Maritime Union (New York), the International Longshoremen's and Warehousemen's Union, centred on San Francisco and responsible for dockside strikes in 1934 and 1936 and the United Office and Professional Workers' Union. The unions formed among the airline employees belong to the CIO, as do many of the miscellaneous unions centred upon New York.

Dating from much the same period (1936) is the International Union, United Automobile, Aircraft and Agricultural Implement Workers of America (UAW), originally formed among the employees of General Motors at Flint, Michigan. After a successful strike in 1937 the UAW went on to unionize the Ford works in 1941 and strike once more against General Motors for 113 days in 1945–6. Like the steelworkers, the members of the UAW have brought a number of other unions into a wider alliance called the American Federation of Labor (AF of L) which covers the building trades, teachers, nurses, clerks and cooks. It is supposed to be less extreme than the CIO but includes the Sailors' Union of the Pacific, the Seamen's International Union and the once disorderly International Alliance of Theatrical and Stage Employees of Hollywood. The famous Teamsters' Union, another affiliate, is strong in the Pacific Northwest, where the Boeing aircraft workers are also affiliated to the AF of L. Attached to the same nationwide organization are the New York tugboat crews who paralysed that city in 1946, and the bricklayers, plasterers and plumbers. In some parts of the USA there was for years some form of alliance between members of the CIO and the AF of L, but elsewhere they were not on speaking terms until they made a formal alliance in 1955. This is one reason for the American failure to produce anything like the British Labour Party.

As compared with left-wing movements in other countries, the US trade union movement is peculiar in three respects. In the first place, the majority of the union members are not opposed to capitalism, nor indeed to big business. Some unions are in business themselves and one of them, the International Ladies' Garment Workers' Union (of New York), went so far as to produce a musical comedy called *Pins and Needles*, which became a hit on Broadway. Most of the union members are satisfied with the world as it is. They know that it is the big corporation which pays them their high wages and they are merely intent on ensuring that it pays them as much as it can afford. They have no desire, in general, to overturn society. In the second place, they model their union on the big business with which its officials are to negotiate. More than in Europe they like to see their union head office as the outward symbol of power, a hive of activity with a staff to be numbered in hundreds. On the same principle they see no reason to underpay their top executives. To put their top-flight negotiators on a level with the employers they must be paid a top executive salary. If their secretary-general has a fine lakeside home with a two-car garage, it proves that their union is prosperous, well organized and influential. In the third place, the US union relates more nearly to industry as it is actually organized. Generally speaking, the directors of General Motors have only the one union with which to negotiate. They do not have the nightmare situation which exists at Dagenham. A Ford electrician in Detroit is in the automobile

industry, he is not an electrician allied to every other electrician in every other factory. This situation does not prevent industrial dispute but it does go some way towards it. The negotiations are tough but the agreement made is usually observed.

Big business has had to respond to the big trade union and it has done so in two ways: through the employers' association and through its own personnel staff. In some industries the employers' association is as old as the union, and Adam Smith, for one, argued that employers' associations, on an informal basis, are probably older. Be that as it may, they are not to be ignored. They represent, moreover, an interesting phenomenon. Industrialists who are engaged in relentless competition with each other, striving for a greater share of the market, are ready to sink their differences in the face of industrial dispute. The keenest rivals and bitterest enemies will come together round the conference table and agree on resistance, compromise, or surrender. When we consider, therefore, the vast authority wielded by a captain of industry, we do well to remember that it may be limited in one direction by trade union opposition and in another by policies agreed among employers for the industry as a whole.

Employers' associations tend to date from the beginning of the century, the Swedish Employers' Confederation being founded in 1902 and the Central Federation of German Manufacturers in 1904. In other countries the associations extend only to a single industry, the national organizations coming later. In Britain the employers did not come together on a national basis until 1965, when three established associations agreed to merge in the present Confederation of British Industries. This co-exists with older and more specialized associations like the Engineering Employers' Federation, the British Federation of Master Printers, the Newspaper Publishers' Association or the complex and ramifying National Federation of Building Trades Employers.

The other response to trade unionism is through the personnel manager. In times past, when the factory was small, the good manager knew his men as individuals. If there was unrest, he knew about it at once or, more probably, sensed it beforehand. In the world of big business these personal contacts have become impossible. There is no time for them. So the company's relationship with its labour force is made the task of a separate department which is concerned, in effect, with nothing else. For purposes of large-scale employment people become personnel, their peculiarities described in a card

OPPOSITE The Confederation of British Industry is the main employers' association in Great Britain. This photograph was taken in 1968 during a visit of the Queen and Prince Philip. With them are (*left*) John Davis, the then director-general of the CBI and (*right*) Sir Stephen Brown KBE, the then president.

Firms like Rowntree's employed women extensively in their cocoa works, although it was not until the First World War that the employment of women became widespread. This photograph, taken in 1900, shows Rowntree factory girls taking their lunch break.

index, their competence pricked on a graph. The first specialists in personnel management were philanthropic employers who took a special interest in this side of their work, realizing that contented people do better work. The pioneer was Robert Owen and later exponents in Britain were Lord Leverhulme (1851–1925), George Cadbury (1839–1922) and Joseph Rowntree (1836–1925). A pioneer in the USA was A. Lincoln Filene, president of a famous department store in Boston, Mass, whose aim was to take all his employees into partnership. His innovations were in profit-sharing and industrial democracy and he described them at length in his book *A Merchant's Horizon* (1924). These ideas were and are of undoubted value but were more applicable to a department store than to an automobile works and more applicable in 1924 than today. Establishments are now on a different scale and the problems involved have become more complex. These are reserved for the personnel manager, who first appears in history in about 1913, described however, as a welfare worker. From that year dates what has since become the (British) Institute of Personnel Management.

In the early days the weakness of the personnel manager resulted from his own relatively humble status. The first welfare workers were women and they were first to be found in firms like Rowntree's Cocoa Works where women were extensively employed. They multiplied during the First World War as the employment of women became more general, and then widened their activities to cover the factory as a whole. Even quite recently, however, the personnel manager has been low in the organization, mainly because of his ignorance of the work being done. In an insurance company the professional members of the board will be insurance men just as they will be engineers in a firm of contractors. Until very recently the personnel manager could seek promotion only by moving in the same capacity to another and larger firm. Things are changing, however, and there are instances today of personnel managers being given a directorship. This is in tacit recognition of the fact that recruitment and selection may be as important as marketing or finance. In the details, therefore, of complaints and fringe benefits, the worker is seldom confronted by the boss or departmental chief but more often by a personnel officer who has been specially trained and is expressly qualified in personnel management. There is now an impressive library in this field, with volumes written on human groups, job analysis, interviewing, incentive payments and trade union law, most of them published during the last decade. One of the current problems in big business is to assure the individual, confronted as he is by a vast and monolithic beehive, that he is still a person and not merely a serial number. This is an exercise in applied psychology, usually well-meant but not invariably successful.

In confrontations between management and trade union the role of the personnel manager is less firmly established. There are two opposing views, both well supported: one, that the general manager should negotiate, the other that the personnel manager should represent the general manager's point of view. One authority on this subject, T. P. Lyons (negotiator of the 'Ilford Agreement'), holds that both these views are wrong. He points out that the personnel manager who is thrust aside at the crucial meeting, and who might have done better on his own, will still have the task of implementing and maintaining the agreement – a task made no easier by the fact that he was himself perhaps opposed to it. He also believes that a true negotiation is impossible if either side must refer back constantly to higher authority:

The personnel role becomes much more logical and final if the function is represented at board or equivalent level, so that ... what is possible and what is desirable are known by the personnel officer who negotiates, and so that the head of the personnel, when he personally takes part – as he would in major matters – can speak and act as the member of top management designated to represent the company ... This amounts to a

'To put it frankly, Mr Morgan, I don't feel I'm getting my fair share of the gravy.' A cartoonist's way of expressing an old complaint.

statement of the view that the head of the personnel function should be able to commit the company and to do so up to limits which he knows by virtue of being a member of the top management.[3]

It is this view which seems likely to prevail in the years to come, providing big business with a useful cushion against the impact of the big unions. In so far, moreover, as unions usually seek and sometimes gain a measure of public sympathy, the directors often feel obliged to appoint a public relations officer (or department) whose duty it will be to present the firm's activities in a favourable light. In this way they provide themselves with a second cushion, placed to meet pressure from a different direction. It would be wrong, of course, to assume that the PR function is as narrowly defensive as that. It can be used for other and more constructive purposes and there are new worlds, no doubt, for the PR man to conquer. But there are those who question his usefulness and one critic, himself a leading industrialist, has gone so far as to head a chapter with the words 'PR Department; Abolition of', and he continues:

Most businesses have a normal PR operation: press releases, clipping services, attempts to get interviewed; all being handled, as usual, by people who are embarrassingly uninformed about the company's plans and objectives.[4]

His remedy is to sack the lot, which, under his exceptional presidency, was probably the right answer. Other people with rather less self-confidence may feel that they want all the support they can find and in every form. For them it will be consoling to know that there are professional propagandists at work on their behalf. The modern equivalent of a good conscience may be a good public image, something for which we shall have to pay. Can this be justified? If it helps to avert industrial dispute, it possibly can.

In conclusion, it may be argued that the big business invites the big strike. The US and Canadian examples seem to show this. As against that, two other related facts are apparent. First, even more days are lost through industrial dispute in Italy, a country where small firms still predominate; and the peace record is as unimpressive in countries like Ireland and Denmark where quite different conditions prevail. Second, if we suppose that large-scale industry makes for unrest, the nationalized industry is plainly no more immune from trouble than the industry run for profit. If there is any definite conclusion to be drawn from the figures available, it would be that small countries have a better record than large, irrespective of the size of firm or the extent to which industry has been nationalized. To this rule Belgium is the exception but with such wild variations from year to year that it may be that the unrest there is more political than economic. Taking the days lost through industrial dispute per thousand persons employed, the Belgian figure for 1957 is as high as 1,471, for 1965 as low as twenty-five. Such figures seem to prove nothing, and if the equivalent figure for Sweden stands at an average of 1.4 we need not

jump to the conclusion that socialism averts strife. For the average return from Switzerland, a capitalist country, stands lower still at 0.1 and points to the opposite conclusion. If these statistics leave us with any impression, it can only be that big business neither promotes nor prevents industrial dispute and that our present troubles throughout the world are more political than our economists can be made to realize.

Business enterprises can be affected by political decisions but these are often based on anything but economic motives. When we come to study the pattern of government interference we shall not find a consistent pattern. Medieval laws on prices and business practices are part of a thread running through economic history. Even in the heyday of capitalism, even in the coarse, unfettered days of early US industrial expansion, the hand of the public authority was never withdrawn. From the colonial period of their history the American colonies had derived a concept of free enterprise and competition. From the American Revolution they had derived a concept of republican equality which led the colonies to adopt a form of democracy in about 1840. Fifty years later the phenomenon of big business left many Americans in a state of mental conflict. Their doctrine of free enterprise was at war with their doctrine of equality. Some means had to be found of reconciling the two ideas. It was felt that government should interfere but it was not easy to decide on the form which such an interference should take.

In their less realistic moments business men will sometimes dream of an economy free from governmental interference. They are tempted to think that all would be well if the government would confine itself to maintaining law and order, leaving commerce and industry to be managed by merchants and manufacturers. There may even have been a moment of eighteenth-century history when such an argument might have seemed almost plausible. But that eighteenth-century dream had nothing to do with the rise of big business.

In Vanderbilt's epic life story the various authorities – federal, state and municipal – were involved from the outset. How could it have been otherwise? The construction of a railway begins with legislation involving the compulsory purchase of land. Grand Central Station in New York is Vanderbilt's monument but it does not commemorate free private enterprise so much as an outstanding success in political manipulation. Tremendous financial risks were run by the men whose railways crossed the continent but they had also

OPPOSITE
'ENOUGH ROPE?'
A cartoon drawn when the fate of the shipbuilding industry on the Upper Clyde hung in the balance. Angered by the Government's decision to close down the industry because it was uneconomic, the unions decided to run it independently.

obtained enormous grants of land. Without government intervention, without a transport system, big business could not have come into existence.

It was not unreasonable, therefore, that government should interfere, as it had always done. The problem posed by big business was to decide how, and the answer to this has varied. In the USA the process probably began very tentatively with the Inter-State Commerce act of 1887, which set up a federal commission to control the railways. Congress might have followed this up by creating a federal commission to deal with monopolies. It chose instead to pass the Sherman Anti-Trust act of 1890 under which 'every contract, combination in the form of trust or otherwise, or conspiracy in restraint of trade ... is hereby declared to be illegal', and 'every person who shall monopolize or combine or conspire with any other person or persons to monopolize any part of the trade or commerce among the several States, or with foreign nations, shall be liable to fine, imprisonment or both.' The intention of this act may have been clear but the words used were not, with the result that the law was ineffective for the next ten years. It was left to the federal courts to find a precise meaning for the word 'monopoly' and indeed for the phrase 'among the several States', and a case brought against E.C. Knight & Co in 1895 failed because the monopoly was merely in the one state of Pennsylvania. These and other dubious phrases were elucidated, however, during the Standard Oil case of 1911, and further clarified by the Clayton Anti-Trust act of 1914. Since then there has been in the USA a fairly consistent effort to discourage monopoly, but that was weakened for a time by the Supreme Court's acquittal of US Steel in 1920. Nevertheless, as E.V. Rostow points out:

... The monopolies of the turn of the century have all disappeared, often in response to direct action under the anti-trust laws. Several studies of the degree of concentration in the American economy show a rough balance between the forces making for monopoly, and those making for more competition ... It is apparent to any observer that the law has denied to American industry some of the easy and efficient forms of open collusion in price making ... and that it has forced business men interested in collusion to retreat to less obvious, and often less workable, procedures of co-operation.[5]

The story then is of legal restraints on big business imposed in the USA during the early years of the present century, and since upheld with a fair but variable amount of success. The British story begins with the same common law objection to a 'conspiracy in distraint of trade' but is otherwise entirely different. There was agitation in Britain against employers, especially during periods of trade recession, but no special concern about monopoly. There were few big combines in Britain anyway, and their power was balanced against other and older institutions. As for the Labour Party, to some degree it welcomed the concentration of industry, as a first step towards public ownership. The sequence of events might have been different, however, but for the impact of the world wars. In both these conflicts the USA played a part, but not in such a way as to commit the entire nation to a desperate and total effort. In Britain the effect of war was momentous, drastic and largely permanent. To win the First World War it became necessary to form a Manpower Board, a Ministry of Munitions and a Ministry of Labour. Essential supplies of iron and coal came under government control and so did merchant shipping, the railways and the nation's food supply. The scope of government activity was widened first by the Ministries of Labour and Pensions, and again in 1919 by the Ministries of Transport and Health. Industrialists themselves were encouraged to form associations which were co-operative rather than competitive. Meanwhile in the background the great socialist thinker Sidney Webb (later Lord Passfield) was planning how to transform wartime improvisations into permanent change. His *War Aims of the Labour Movement* were agreed by the party in 1917 and led to the more detailed manifesto of 1918. In this the party committed itself to attempting 'a systematic approach towards a healthy equality of material circumstances for every person born into the world'. This would involve a reorganization of industry on the basis of the 'common ownership of the means of production'. It would imply, more immediately, the total nationalization of land, railways, shipping, mines and electricity plants. Wartime conditions indicated the scope of nationalization and the wartime mood had eliminated all thought of cost. Once we have accepted the view that munitions must be made available regardless of expense it is easy to accept that the same reasoning can apply to hospitals, houses and schools. Sidney Webb's plan has been accepted policy for fifty years and much of it has been carried out, largely by his political opponents. A first step towards achieving this programme of nationalization was an act of 1921, the work of Sir Eric Geddes, which reduced the number of railway companies to four.

Reorganization of the railways had proved essential for the wartime period of government control, but this so raised wages and reduced hours of work that the pre-war companies were no longer economically viable. Each railway group might now be regarded as a big, if dying, business but the element of competition, so dear to US theorists, had been more or less abolished.

The process tentatively begun during the First World War was largely completed during and after the Second World War. In that conflict there was a still more complete and centralized organization of the national war effort. It is interesting to reflect that the German commitment to the war was never as complete as that of the British. As late as July 1944, Albert Speer was still imploring Hitler to remedy the chaotic deployment of manpower and even to order a survey of how German manpower had been actually allocated. By comparison with the Germans, the British were ruthless and efficient. While all

this deployment took place, the Labour Party planners used their opportunity as they had done during the First World War. When war ended and the peace brought them into office, their plans were made. These resulted in the Coal Industry Nationalization act of 1946, the Electricity act of 1947, the Transport act of 1947, the Gas act of the same year, and the Iron and Steel act of 1949. So far as big business went in Britain, a number of industries were put out of reach. Two of them (railways and coal) were already bankrupt and ripe for subsidy at the taxpayer's expense. Electricity and gas had been largely municipal, and were now to be more centralized. Controversy centred upon the Iron and Steel act, for the steel industry was at least theoretically capable of paying a dividend. At that point the nationalization campaign came to a halt, although a Labour Party publication of 1949 included proposals for the nationalization of industrial insurance, the manufacture of sugar, the cement industry and the

Women war workers in an engineering shop in 1917. During the Second World War labour became deployed in Great Britain more ruthlessly than ever before.

'. . . subject of course to
no pilots' strike, no ground
staff strike, no Tube
strike. . . .' A cartoonist's
view of the British
industrial situation.

water supply. Socialists had by then resigned themselves to the idea
of a mixed economy, to 'an effective partnership' between government
and industry. Even Aneurin Bevin had reached the conclusion that
'the victory of socialism need not be universal to be decisive'.

But what partnership could there be between two managerial groups,
one of them publicly committed to the destruction of the other? And
what inspiration was to be derived from the current state of industries
that had been brought into public ownership? If the railwaymen
and miners had seen themselves as the spearhead of a great movement
and had thrown themselves into frenzied activity, registering their joy
at serving the community and showing their relief at being free of the
selfish capitalists, there would have been a strong case for nationalizing
cement and sugar. But neither British Rail nor the Coal Board could
point to any dramatic change in atmosphere, still less to any
improvement in efficiency. All that the experiment proved was that

workers in an obsolescent and dying industry are more likely to go on strike than are those in an industry which can look to the future. All reason would suggest that people living under the threat of unemployment should recoil from any actions which would bring them into the news. Experience proves the opposite, that low morale leads to industrial dispute and that nationalization makes no difference one way or the other.

Big business in Britain had been mostly left, meanwhile, to its own devices. There were complaints about monopoly and profiteering after the First World War and there was even a committee on trusts. But the Monopolies Bill, drafted in 1920, came to nothing. With at least tacit government approval the leading chemical firms merged in 1926 to form Imperial Chemical Industries. Unilever was formed in 1929. The Dunlop Rubber Company merged with the Charles Mackintosh group in 1925. Morris Motors acquired the Wolseley Company in 1927 and the rise of English Electric dates from the same period. While the evolving pattern was not one of actual monopoly it was certainly one which established a market leader in a number of the more profitable industries. Nor was this a matter for public concern:

On the eve of the Second World War, indeed, public opinion, government policy and the law, far from holding monopolies and restrictive practices in disfavour, had moved to their support, and the retreat from competition among manufacturers and traders was widely regarded as a traditional stage in the creation of a nationally ordered or planned economy.[6]

This trend towards monopoly was given fresh impetus during the Second World War. For war purposes many industries were nationalized. The allocation of raw materials combined with rationing and price control to end competition and bring factories under the supervision of trade associations which were themselves merely agents of government. What had been a wartime expedient was made more permanent by the Industrial Organisation and Development act of 1947, the purpose of which was to strengthen those trade associations and move further towards a planned economy with output restricted and prices fixed. The complacency with which the leading firms accepted this situation was enough, however, to give some people second thoughts. How would such protected industries fare in competition against US and European rivals? Enough doubt was expressed to ensure the enactment of the Monopolies and

Restrictive Practices act of 1948. This was the first British attempt in modern times to deal with the monopoly problem. It might seem, at first sight, a reversal of administrative attitudes but the act was less decisive than that. Its effect was to set up a Monopolies Commission to investigate allegations of monopoly and advise the government whether any given situation was or was not contrary to the public interest. This commission did intervene from time to time and its existence had a wider influence than its actual history would prove. It also produced a general report which led to the Restrictive Trade Practices act of 1956, under which trade associations lost their price-maintaining function. Under the same act there was also set up a Restrictive Practices Court and a Register of Restrictive Trading Agreements. Enough was done to demonstrate that agreements between manufacturers might incur official disapproval. Little was done, by contrast, to prevent actual mergers.

'We must intensify our efforts to put a stop to the crippling effects of restrictive practices.'

It so happens that Britain had a spate of merger activity between 1953 and 1958. It began with Harold Samuel's unsuccessful attempt to take over the Savoy Group, continued with the GUS acquisition of Hope Brothers and the Rootes' takeover of Singer, and ended for the time being with Charles Clore's conquest of J. Sears and Hugh Fraser's acquisition of Harrod's. Much alarm was expressed at the time, and the immediate result was the publication of a suggested take-over code in 1959. This was a document approved by key institutions in the city, including the stock exchange, urging (among other things) that a shareholder should be given all the relevant information. There followed another code, published this time by the Board of Trade, and again in the form of recommendation rather than injunction. It was clear, however, that each case should be considered on its merits. A realization of this fact could have led to the establishment of another industrial court but the city authorities took the initiative, setting

up the Takeover Panel under Lord Shawcross and Ian Fraser. It was
never the intention that mergers would be restrained by this device
but it would seem that the Panel has had great success in discouraging
the sort of operation in which the shareholders' interests can be
largely ignored. This first merger period is well described by George
Bull and Anthony Vice in their book *Bid for Power* (London 1958),
the third edition of which was revised and updated in 1961.

Britain was a largely socialist country from 1945 and so remained
under a supposedly conservative government from 1951 to 1964.
There was a planned economy, with much money being spent by the
National Research and Development Corporation and much activity
under the Distribution of Industry act. Collusion and price-fixing
continued, however, and led to the Restrictive Trade Practices act of
1956. There was little in this to discourage mergers and the
Conservatives were still pondering over this problem when they went
out of office. It was left to a Labour government to reform the economy
after 1964. The socialist effort began with setting up the Ministry of
Technology and the Department of Economic Affairs and took
firmer shape in the Monopolies and Mergers act of 1965. This
empowered the Board of Trade to forbid mergers or dissolve existing
monopolies on the advice of the commission. An early subject for
investigation was Courtauld's invasion of the cotton industry, which
was checked though not prevented. By contrast, Pilkington's move
towards monopoly in the glass industry was approved, on some
principle which is not immediately apparent. Alarm was expressed,
by contrast, on both sides of the House, when the US Chrysler firm
acquired a large share in Rootes, the British motor manufacturers.
Future prosperity was to be guaranteed, nevertheless, by the Labour
Party's National Economic Plan for 1970, announced to a spellbound
public in 1965. 'This plan, which failed even as a statistical exercise,
deserves to be restored, with the minimum of comment, to the
obscurity from which it ought never to have emerged.'[7]

This is a harsh verdict indeed. Are students of economics never to
be allowed any comic relief?

The background to the next merger boom (1966–9) was provided
by the government itself. Alarm over the Chrysler-Rootes merger
had persuaded Harold Wilson and his ministers that the best way to
prevent undesirable mergers was to encourage beforehand the sort
of merger which would serve the public interest. This policy led to
the setting up of the Industrial Reorganization Corporation in 1966,

provided with £150 million to assist the rationalization (the merger) of industries considered ripe for such treatment. There was passed that same year the Industrial Development act which was to drive manufacturers into setting up new plants in marginal constituencies or remote areas afflicted with unemployment. From the same busy time dates the Selective Employment Tax, designed to drive labour from the less essential to the more essential industries; a process to be further hastened, no doubt, by the re-nationalization of steel in 1967. If there was an element of confusion in this planning it was introduced by the Restrictive Trade Practices act of 1968, which appeared inconsistent, at first sight, with industrial reorganization. It would be wrong, however, to regard this as a period of mere prohibitions and restraints. On the more constructive side, official subsidies to private industry reached a total of £1,192 million in 1968–9, a quarter as much as was lavished on social security, half as much as was spent on defence. The government thus came to the rescue of firms concerned with aircraft, aluminium, computers and hotels. As for shipbuilders their development plans were covered by a forty-five per cent loan, and their overseas customers were encouraged to place orders by the loan of four hundred million pounds between them at a low rate of interest.

The merger boom which coincided with all this well-meant activity was distinguished, first of all, by the rise of Jim Slater, who acquired control of the Slater Walker industrial group in 1966. Other acquisitions followed in rapid succession, including a moribund firm in Australia with assets worth about £2.25 million acquired at a cost of £1.35 million. Slater then bought Crittall-Hope, the metal window manufacturers and the Drage's group, and so went on to make his bid for Forestal in 1969. That company had been in the leather-tanning business, with properties in Argentina, New York and South and East Africa. With the invention of synthetic leather Forestal began to diversify, moving into health foods and many other things, but lacked capital to build up a new business. Slater bought the company for £10.5 million and sold its assets for £18.1 million, giving Slater-Walker a profit of over seven million pounds. Around the same time a very different kind of merger took place between Cadbury and Schweppes – not in order to sell assets at a profit, but to plan for long-term co-operation in the food business. From an historical point of view the marriage between the old philanthropic Quaker firm, and the manufacturers of the tonic which goes with the gin was somewhat incongruous, but both had moved into food products and there were some useful economies to be made in both manufacturing and marketing.

The government had no part in either of these mergers but was directly concerned in two others which were of greater importance. The first was the merger of General Electric with the English Electric

Company in 1968. GEC had been transformed during the previous years by Sir Arnold Weinstock, who placed it in a strong financial position. After taking over AEI, Weinstock made a bid for English Electric. The point of interest in this move is that it had the blessing of the Industrial Reorganization Corporation. It was immediately followed by the even more significant takeover by Leyland of the

Big business and pollution: the Friends of the Earth stage a demonstration outside Schweppes' offices to protest about the manufacture of non-returnable bottles. FAR LEFT the beginning of the protest and LEFT the morning after.

British Motor Corporation, itself the result of the merger of Morris and Austin in 1952. A previous and important event had been the Chrysler-Rootes alliance which introduced into Britain a new element of US competition. It was this which convinced the Labour Government that a merger of BMC and Leyland offered the best hope of keeping British cars in the world market.

Why were Labour ministers so keen on the merger? There were basically two reasons. One was that at that stage the Labour Cabinet was convinced of the great benefit of mergers to be achieved through economies in production, finance and marketing; above all, ministers were seized with the need for British companies to merge in order to be able to compete with their larger European and US counterparts.[8]

The merger took place and British Leyland (BLMC) was the result, some seventy plants organized in seven divisions, headed by Donald Stokes (now Lord Stokes) and largely financed, as Rootes had been, by the IRC. The problem is now for the new group to compete successfully with its European and US, not to mention Japanese, rivals. It has a falling share of the home market and only a very limited foothold in Europe. Its future must turn on its success within the EEC and this will be a test of Britain itself as an industrial power.

When the Conservatives came to power in 1970 they talked confidently about the need for industries to stand on their own feet. There was to be some necessary reorganization – the Monopolies Commission to amalgamate with the National Board for Prices and Incomes, thus creating the Commision for Industry and Manpower – and no further waste of money on the 'lame ducks'. This business-like attitude lasted less than a year. By 1971 the government had to rescue Rolls Royce, the prestigious manufacturers of aero-engines, and by 1972 it was pouring millions into the less hopeful shipyards on the Clyde, and into Belfast where unemployment provided the background to civil war. Inflation accompanied a continuous discussion about how inflation might be cured but the government succeeded in its central purpose, which was to take Britain into the EEC. Whatever the theory may be of conservative government, its actual practice is socialist, nor is there any immediate prospect of it changing in character. The government is too deeply committed to its role in industry, especially through loans and investments, to assume any credible role as umpire. There may be continued lip service to the value of healthy competition but recently even the two state-owned airlines, BOAC and BEA have merged. The government's domination of the national economy is now a fact and the part played by big business, except in partnership with government, is both limited and dwindling. This situation would be less unnerving if government policy were more consistent (and more successful) than it usually seems to be.

It is easy to deride the politician who plunges into business, thumbing his Oxford lecture notes and taking the advice of Hungarian exiles, but his policy is not based on mere ignorance. His weakness is rather one inherent in democracy. He cannot observe the stern discipline of finance, because unemployment will lose him votes. The decisions he makes are sometimes not even business decisions, least of all when they attempt to influence the location of industry. In times past the industrialist wanted to be near his sources of raw material, iron ore, wool or coal. Today, especially in lighter industries, he may want to be near his market. But the politician of either party will urge or compel him to site his plant where employment is needed. A classic example of this is provided by the story of Rootes before its takeover by Chrysler. In planning the production of the Hillman Imp the directors wanted to site the new factory near Dunstable. They were persuaded by the government to build this plant at Linwood in Renfrewshire, part of the same regional policy which brought Vauxhall, Ford and Triumph into Lancashire. Rootes had therefore to employ an unskilled labour force with a bad record for industrial unrest. The Linwood project was a financial disaster and a chief factor in Rootes' collapse. This is but one instance of a business decision influenced by political considerations. Similar decisions have been fairly numerous and the taxpayer has to meet the cost. The point is however that these decisions are politically unavoidable, just as are the losses in a nationalized industry. The price of democracy is inflation.

It is a question today whether the trend of technology leaves room for the freedom of industry. Projects like Concorde, whether wise or not, are beyond the scope of what used to be private enterprise. Even the USA affords proof of this in some directions, although Wall Street largely retains its independence. This was illustrated in 1969 by Leasco's attempt to take over the Chemical Bank of New York. The Leasco Data Processing Equipment Corporation was legally incorporated in 1965, a computer leasing business founded by Saul

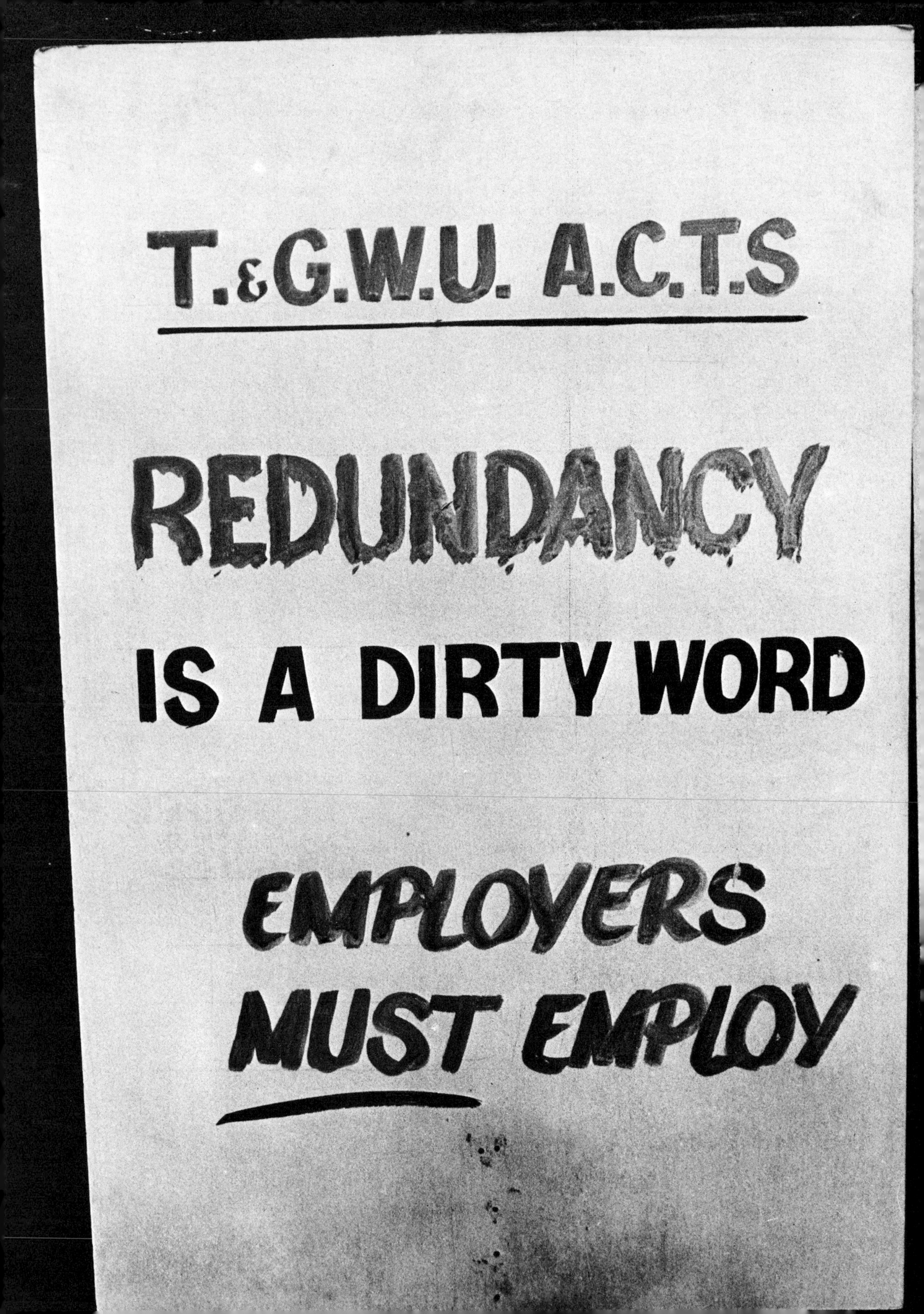
T.&G.W.U. A.C.T.S
REDUNDANCY
IS A DIRTY WORD
EMPLOYERS
MUST EMPLOY

Steinberg with a total staff of seventeen. The business grew and diversified and Steinberg took over various other firms including, finally in 1968, the Reliance Insurance Company of Philadelphia. Leasco assets now reach a thousand million dollars and Steinberg, with 8,500 employees, did business in fifty countries. He began secretly to buy up shares in the Chemical Bank of New York with a view to its takeover. The president of the bank became aware of this and planned a defensive campaign and indeed a counter-attack. The result of his various counter-moves was that Leasco shares began to fall in value. No less than 378,100 shares were sold in under three weeks due to the action of major investment funds. One thing clear was that the Leasco attempt was regarded with 'negative enthusiasm' in banking circles and that the Chemical Bank had more friends than Steinberg had realized. When the bid was withdrawn Steinberg made the memorable comment 'I always knew there was an establishment. I just used to think I was part of it'. Such an incident in Britain would have ended with government intervention. In Wall Street the takeover was prevented by a general disapproval of what was being threatened. But even there the possibility of federal intervention was not remote. What can still be claimed for Wall Street, nevertheless, is that the federal government is at least in another city.

Some attempt has been made in this chapter to outline the restraints on big business imposed in the USA and Britain by law, by administration and by opinion. No mention has been made, however, of the most important intervention of all. For governments which have been indecisive and wavering in their attitudes towards monopoly have been consistent in their levying of taxes. In each country's modern history the one certainty has been that taxes will become heavier each decade and that any tax abolished will be promptly replaced by something worse. Taxation of this twentieth-century pattern, rising to reach and exceed the point of self-defeat, is a normal and probably inevitable result of democracy. When it falls on firms it is normally passed on again to the customer, who thus pays a heavier tax than he is allowed to know. When it falls on individuals it does so most heavily on salaried people whose incomes are precisely known. Its effect on big business becomes important only when it is imposed on capital gains. It was at first a principle of direct taxation both in Britain and the USA that income is taxable and that capital is not, an exception to this rule taking the form of estate duty payable on decease. 'Death duties', introduced by Sir William Harcourt in 1893, infringe a basic

OPPOSITE One of the posters which appeared during the unions' demonstration against the Industrial Relations Bill.

Big business and pollution: *'It's to meet the Trades' Description Act.'* This act has prevented some big businesses from going their own sweet way.

principle by confusing capital with income. They have tended, nevertheless, to break up the larger estates, and legislation now impending in Britain will strengthen that tendency. Capital gains are taxable in both Britain and the USA but on a lower scale than income. The final pattern of taxation is a complex one, far too involved for discussion here, and yet impossible to ignore. It is an important aspect of big business, so important that many business decisions are distorted by tax considerations. For present purposes we have merely to remember that the problem exists and that tax avoidance is now a business in its own right, and may even be regarded as big business.

The question of tax avoidance is considered in a fairly recent play, *The Latent Heterosexual*. The central character is an American novelist who has been totally unsuccessful for twenty years, so much so that he has never had to fill a tax return. Then one of his novels is bought by a film company, giving him a vast sum in a single year. The tax authorities promptly conclude that this high figure represents his average income for the last two decades. They demand arrears with interest and penalties, the alternative being a life sentence in a federal penitentiary. The play begins at the point when the distracted author seeks the aid of a leading firm of tax attorneys. They briskly take the obvious step, which is to have him certified as insane. That done, they entrust his literary property and output to a corporation of which he will be president. Still further to strengthen his position they decide that he should create and preside over a charitable foundation. He is by then a mere puppet in their hands, his prosperity assured but his freedom gone. He must now marry, they agree (purely for tax purposes), partly with a view to securing the tax advantages which will result from the subsequent divorce. Further developments are not of purely fiscal interest but the plot is one from which many valuable lessons may be learnt. In the light of this instruction we can be sure that even big business has its lunatic fringe. This is provided by the government and is one of the services with which we are supplied at our own expense. In the welfare state we are taught to look to the government for all our needs and, not least, for comic relief.

ALUE AND FUTURE OF BIG BUSINESS

The background to our daily lives is largely the creation of big business. Nature may provide the earth, the air and the daylight but much else of what we see and feel has been manufactured and mass-produced. We rise each day to apply a brushless shaving cream and shave with a stainless steel razor blade. We breakfast on coffee and corn-flakes, listen to the radio as we drive to the office in a petrol-driven and rubber-tyred car and presently have our letters typed on an electric typewriter. We can thus barely begin the day without using the services of Colgate-Palmolive, Wilkinson, Kellogg, Nestlé, GEC, Standard Oil, General Motors, Dunlop and IBM. There are those who maintain that all this surrounding and ubiquitous equipment is of marginal significance, that our thoughts are our own, that our souls are free. We are, they think, as we should have been in any case, human beings with natural instincts and inherited limitations, men with a spark of divine fire, capable of love, hate and poetry, chained to the earth but reaching for the stars. But is this wholly true? Our ideas as well as our lives are formed by the civilization in which we actually live. Our energies are affected by our diet, our religion by our expectation of life, our morality by our contraceptives, our leg muscles by the automobile, our health by tobacco and our sobriety by gin. We are such stuff as teams are made of, our little lives are much like those of sheep. If we lacked the material aids which surround us, we should not be the people that we are. Is this rank materialism? Many think so, pointing to other activities which seem more idealistic. We have political opinions and cultural aspirations. But are these really divorced from the flat and the car, the weekend cottage and the cabin cruiser? Do they derive – or are they not at least reinforced – by television? Throughout history material factors have been very important indeed. They are more than ever important today.

In considering this material world, many of us see it as the work of human invention and science. We owe the transistor or penicillin, we think, to men of genius. There is a sense in which this is true. Without the inventor's brilliance the transistor would not exist. But we need to realize that no stroke of inventive genius could have brought the transistor radio to our own bedside. That was the achievement of the manufacturer. More than that, it was specifically the achievement of big business, a feat of mass production and cost analysis. It is one thing to devise a transistor radio, quite another to produce a million of them at a price which a million people can afford. The technology behind the telephone is as remarkable as the instrument itself. The idea of the submarine is centuries older than the first vessel of this type, the invention being useless until technology had caught up with it. Where objects of daily use are concerned, the same principle applies, but added to it is the contribution of advertising. Once an appliance or luxury has been invented the procedure is to sell it to the wealthy few, add to it the glamour which attaches to this élite and then so lower the price that the same thing becomes available to all but the poor. As far as consumer goods are concerned, the function of big business is to create a demand and then satisfy it. This is done with tremendous skill and our material surroundings are the result of this process taking place for the last hundred years and especially the last fifty. When we study this transformation of our lives, with its profound effects on character and health and energy, we are unavoidably impressed by the efficiency of big business. Whatever we think of the end result, the process represents a triumph of forethought, planning, imagination and competence. We have reason to assume that the process will continue on a still bigger scale and at a faster speed. We may even be tempted, like H.G. Wells, to picture a Utopian future with the world improved and beautified by science.

Unfortunately for our Utopian dreams we soon come to realize that progress in science and technology has not been accompanied by any comparable progress in politics. All our political ideas date from the days of the horse-drawn vehicle and our political institutions have not developed usefully since the present century began. As for our political behaviour, it has in fact deteriorated, leaving us with a growing sense of disorder, confusion and collapse. And this is the problem with which we are confronted: a problem which results from the appalling contrast between the competence of our industry and the abysmal inefficiency of our political systems, concepts and leadership. It is easy to mock the democratic politicians of our day, unable as they are to see the problem, let alone solve it. But the fact is that the men are often better than the system they must follow, and wiser than the political principles to which they are supposedly dedicated. We must also remember that the task of the politician is infinitely more complex than the task of the industrialist. The manufacturer seeks to market something at a profit. To that one simple purpose he devotes a wealth of knowledge, experience and skill. Calling to his aid the scientist, the engineer, the psychologist and designer, he produces what is useful or anyway desirable and proves that it is essential. Nothing could be more impressive and no human talent could have used more effective means to achieve a given result. But the impressiveness of the means applied must not blind us to the fact that the task was relatively easy. There may have been technical and legal difficulties, sales resistance and competition, but the aim at least was never in doubt. For the politician the aim is as much in dispute as the means. His policy is confused, moreover, by a hundred changing influences – religious, economic, racial, local – and the final decision is at best a compromise, at worst a mere postponement. The central problem of the future in the USA and Europe is somehow to reconcile the competence of big business with the ineffectiveness of politics.

This reconciliation is no easy task in any circumstances but its attainment is further hindered by the fact that politics and big business are no longer even geographically related. The political unit in the world of today is the nation state as created and defined by the warfare of the past. The effective nation was the largest populated area which could be brought into a measure of military, linguistic and economic cohesion. Were it too extensive, like Austria-Hungary, it fell apart. Were it too small, like Scotland, it was usually annexed by its neighbour. Looking back after receiving the benefit of a patriotic education, we tend to assume that nations are what they are inevitably, that they had always existed in popular sentiment and had only to gain identity and a defined frontier in order to achieve political recognition. The process was, however, less certain than that and the results more haphazard. Why should Norway and Denmark be different countries? Why is Portugal detached from Spain? Why does Indonesia include Sumatra or Great Britain include Wales? There are many questions we may ask but the most obvious result of nationalism is to make a reality of the frontier which has been accidentally attained. Once the line is drawn on the map the forces of law and language, of literature and education, will be loosed on the peoples concerned. Whatever their original similarity, they will acquire sharp differences of character and culture, diverging on either side of a single strand of barbed wire. By now the frontiers seem as real to the schoolboy as the mountains and rivers, and these provide the framework within which our political institutions are arranged. It is only with an effort that we can realize that they are not eternal. They did not exist from the beginning of time and they need not exist for ever. We are reminded of this when we see new nations coming into existence in India or Africa. We can also observe the process by which they fail to achieve nationality or lose what nationality they had. Frontiers within Britain were once as doubtful as those of Bangladesh or Biafra.

Accidental as many of these frontiers may be, they do gain reality from the passage of time. And these frontiers do not relate to the world of big business or indeed to the world of business at all. The multinational companies have long since outgrown their countries of origin, Switzerland being dwarfed by Nestlé and the Netherlands by Unilever and Shell. Moreover, it is clear that the companies are growing in size, and that their multinational character is gaining emphasis. They are not within the political framework. They overshadow it. The question we have to answer is: how to reconcile political theory with economic fact? And the basis of our discussion must be the realization that the trade route is a reality and the frontier a fiction. It may not be impossible to enthrone fiction as the ultimate truth but the result is usually unstable. Balanced on its apex, the pyramid will fall down on its flat. Human affairs must tend towards stability and this should convince us that the internationalism of big business should mostly prevail over the nationalism that is the basis of our politics. There are reasons for hoping that big business should thus succeed – reasons connected with war and nuclear physics – and here our hopes and expectations may coincide. It is easy to recognize the defects of nationalism in the old-established countries of Europe and easier still to recognize them as caricatured in the supposedly developing nations which have only recently appeared on the map.

Countries ruled by a comic-opera dictatorship are unfavourable to business in that they are at once unstable and obsolete. We do wrong, however, to suppose that a reversion to democracy would improve them. It is the tendency of democracy to turn into socialism, and it is the habit of socialists to nationalize industry. Much could be said about the results of nationalization but our immediate concern is with its cause. For the process of nationalization is a very narrow one. The industry which comes under government control loses overnight all trace of international character. Britain's nationalized steel and coal industries are run for the profit, in theory, of the government and for the convenience, in practice, of the men they employ. But the scope of their enterprise (if 'enterprise' is the term to use) ends at the frontier and must never stray beyond it. What has been nationalized has become in effect parochial. Socialism is thus the very antithesis of internationalism. There are conferences, no doubt, at which there is talk of the brotherhood of man. But the socialists' real aim is to keep the trade within the country and exclude the foreigner. Their favourite target is the company with overseas plants at which foreign labour is employed. At moments of crisis, as when industrial dispute coincides with war, socialists are sometimes said to be unpatriotic. This is normally quite untrue. Their plan is always to strengthen and extend the functions of government, as must normally happen in wartime, and so restrain the industrialist's tendency to make friends with aliens who chance to be in the same line of business. Big business is a step towards international co-operation. Socialism is a step in the other direction.

There is then a real difficulty in reconciling the aims of government and big business. The politician's concern is with his constituents, his party and his country. In a democracy he will not be re-elected if he shows interest in anything else. His platform and mandate are solely concerned with the welfare of the voters and he has publicly pledged himself to do his utmost for them. He may have uttered a few platitudes about world peace and the United Nations, but these will have been accepted as no more than ritual. His real commitment is to the voters' standard of living. The chairman of Standard Oil of New Jersey has a different set of loyalties. He must try to provide his share-holders with a fair dividend. He must manufacture and market a range of oil products and derivatives, all fit to use for their purpose and safe to handle in the meanwhile. He must provide salaries and wages for all who are employed by the group. He must plan to make other and better products in course of time, holding and preferably increasing his share of the market. And none of these basic aims has anything to do with the USA or New Jersey, the shareholders and employees being scattered all over the world. Any reconciliation, therefore, of big business and government can take only one form: a more international form of government. There is no real alternative because the firms in big business are international or multinational already and to make them more national would be to destroy them. It

is the governments that will have to change and this will mean an end to democracy in its present form. One cannot administer on the international level if one's sworn commitment is to the welfare of one's constituents in Dusseldorf, Hartlepool or Portland, Oregon. No union of national governments can form an international government. The union must be one of people who already think internationally.

To say that big business would be destroyed if it were nationalized is obvious. It is less evident, but none the less true, that it can be damaged through being persuaded to follow what are believed to be the national interests. The fact that this is harmful does not mean that no such attempt is being made. It is made continually in Britain, bankers and industrialists being told what they should do in the public

'I only came in for two gallons of Super.' A cartoonist voices popular feelings towards the Arab sheiks.

interest. The word in current use in this context is 'responsible' and pressure is brought to bear upon the industrialist to act so as to combat inflation or create a favourable balance of trade. This means, we are told, to act 'responsibly'. It has been left to Enoch Powell to point out the fallacy of this idea:

It needs to be understood that such actions and attitudes are not only not praiseworthy or patriotic but the reverse. Who made these persons 'responsible' for the national interest? Nobody; they are not in any sense responsible for it. They do not know where it lies; it is not their business to decide where it lies; and they have not been given the right or power to bring about what they deem to be in the national interest. In short they are not called to account, and are not treated as those who are called to account, for their management of the national interest. Their claim, whether they are conscious of the fact or not, is a usurpation. It is no use their pleading: 'but the government told us what the national interest required and we obeyed them.' The excuse makes the offence worse. If the citizen is required to act in the general interest in a particular way, it is lawful authority (which will be held 'responsible' for its judgment) which must command him to do so and, if need be, enforce the command. The requirement cannot be communicated through generalities in a white paper or a speech, or by a nod and a wink across a minister's desk in Whitehall, or by a trade association circular. . . .

The citizen's responsibility, then, as a citizen, is that which the law imposes on him, and neither he nor anyone else can add to this – or only at the cost of destroying freedom under the rule of law.[1]

This argument is conclusive. The board of directors which acts on a hint from the ministry – perhaps against the interests of the share-holders or the employees or both – is exceeding the powers under which it is to act. Such a policy is improper and quite possibly illegal. And the case is strengthened when the company is doing business in several countries. There is then no one government to which the directors need listen. Industry today lies most open to criticism on the score of pollution, and industrialists are urged on all sides to act responsibly and save the environment. But where do they stand if their well-meant efforts should make the situation worse? It is for the legislature to make the laws, for the government to enforce them and for the industrialist to obey them. It is not the task of industry to regulate itself and act 'responsibly'. Exhortation on this subject is misguided and quite possibly dangerous. It is a plausible idea that leaders of industry should practise patriotism and statesmanship but it is no answer to the current problems. We know that major corporations like General Motors have yielded to public pressure in matters of safety and pollution, going far beyond the legal requirement. This sort of 'responsible' policy is the result of an outcry being allowed to have the force of law, and a local outcry at that. But the background of big business is essentially international. It is true that industrial leaders may sometimes respond to political pressure but the practice is not one to be encouraged. The politician's 'nod and wink' is irresponsible and compliance with it may leave the industrialist in the impossible position of having acted against the interests of his firm.

The trend, therefore, of big business is to become more international in outlook and less and less subject to the control of any one

'What happens if Iceland extends her territorial waters again?' North Sea oil is a fabulous investment for Great Britain – but how much of it will she be allowed to keep?

government. We may guess, further, that nationalism is on the wane, especially in Europe, and that the importance of the frontiers is going to lessen. The need will soon arise for a supra-national organization of the multinational firms. This should perhaps take the form of an annual world conference and a more frequent meeting of companies at the continental level, North America being one base for this and Europe another. With this design we should see a new kind of industrial statesmanship and a new kind of industrial diplomacy. The present technological trend would seem to favour a world forum for discussion as well as a world market. This probable development points then to another conclusion. We are sometimes told that the computer is tending to mechanize management. It was suggested as long ago as 1958 that information technology will make centralization much easier and will widen the scope of top management's control. It was also foreseen that while the functions of middle management would become less important, those of top management would be more vital than ever:

As the work of the middle manager is programmed, the top manager should be freed more than ever from internal detail. But the top will not only be released to think; it will be *forced* to think. We doubt that many large companies in the 1980s will be able to survive for even a decade without major changes in products, methods, or internal organization.[2]

This prediction is already in process of fulfilment and a later forecast points to the same conclusion: 'Central staff activities will mushroom at first, as will staff size: then central staff positions will decrease in number but the demands on staff creativity will be higher.'[3]

This is almost certainly true. Data-processing techniques will reduce the areas of guesswork, providing numerical answers to questions of quantity, but this will give added value to the factor which is beyond the scope of the machine. This factor is imagination, which represents the human element at its most precious. In future it seems probable that imagination will be the ultimate secret, the key to success at the highest level. We may also guess that it is the internationalization of business which will introduce the data which cannot be exactly processed. It is through creativity that big business will prosper and from the lack of it that some businesses will fail.

The fact we have to remember is that multinational business brings with it a range of problems which the computer cannot digest. In a recent and important book[4] Nicholas Faith assesses the extent to which the much-publicized US invasion of Europe has been balanced by a less obvious European invasion of the USA. This began even before the First World War with the movement headed by Shell and Unilever, but the more recent invaders have included four Swiss companies, Nestlé, CIBA, Geigy and Hoffman-La Roche, and one Dutch company, AKU. Nestlé, with estimated US sales of $720 million in 1969, owed much of its success to instant coffee, the drug companies to the confiscation of their German rivals in 1942. There have followed still more recently, the successful inroads made by Olivetti, Bowater, Beecham and Schweppes. The figurehead of this movement, so far as Britain was concerned, was Commander Whitehead, who gained a market in the USA for Schweppes Tonic and went on to repeat the trick with Bitter Lemon. What is interesting, in retrospect, is that gin-and-tonic was sold to the world by the makers of the tonic rather than the makers of the gin. Beecham attacked the US market with Brylcreem and Macleans Toothpaste. Bowater sold newsprint on the US market and then moved into British Columbia. Then came the Italian typewriter firm of Olivetti which has become Olivetti-Underwood, going on to market its Programma 101 microcomputer. More surprising is the fact that New York's Pan-Am building, dominating Park Avenue, owes its existence to Jack Cotton and Erwin Wolfson of London. Even this achievement is dwarfed however by BP, the company which struck oil in Alaska in 1969 and then merged with Sinclair Oil and Sohio. The story of these campaigns in the USA, like that of the US campaigns in Europe, is one in which diplomatic skill plays a considerable part. At the top level of big business, and especially in multinational big business, there is great scope for imagination, persuasiveness, politeness and courage. These are qualities of the greatest significance and the computer possesses none of them.

It is probable that big business will claim, as time goes on, a still bigger share of the human talent that is available. But is big business destined to become bigger still? The answer is that it must. The research that underlies the great discoveries, whether geophysical in Alaska or chemical in Mannheim, demands a scale of investment that is beyond the reach of the family firm. In the design and construction of aircraft, for example, the duplication of effort by rival teams must be described in the end as uneconomic. When BAC joins with Hawker-Siddeley we have to admit that the merger is rational. Quite apart from that, there are whole areas of the world where modern industry has still to penetrate. Nationalism is the obstacle but it is likely to give way in the end to the logic of progress. With the breaking down of the national frontiers, the subsidiary companies must multiply and the business empires must extend. If there are limits to industrial expansion it is probably safe to say that we have not reached them. As for the dangers which immediately confront us, these are not due to big business as such but to the fact that our political institutions are obsolete. Our votes and elections, our assemblies and committees are

'. . . and then of course there is our Economy Tour to see which bank is offering the most favourable exchange rates.' A cartoonist's inflation-beating idea.

unrelated to the world in which we actually live. The jet plane belongs to the future, the customs barrier to the past. We see the truth of this when it is caricatured in Ireland, but our own ideas (like socialism) too often belong to the age of the horse-drawn vehicle. Wherever our technology may take us, our politicians lag all too far behind. As this fact becomes increasingly apparent there must be a move to bring the world's business leaders into whatever form of world government there may be, not merely because they have a contribution to make, but because they are too important to be left out. They represent above all much that is contemporary and real. Compared with the great industrial groups our political institutions are many of them antiquated, ineffectual and bogus.

Leadership of the Western nations belongs without question to the USA but centres less upon Washington than upon New York. That is the city which the migrant from Europe is likely to approach, guidebook in hand. As the aircraft lands, a studious immigrant will revise his knowledge once more, memorizing all that he should know about the President and Senate, about the party system and the elections, about democracy, freedom and the rule of law. Driving into the city after sunset with the light fading over Manhattan, he might look about him hopefully, keen to identify City Hall, the cathedral and all the other monuments he might expect to see such as the law courts and the mayor's official residence. Then as he reaches the city itself the lights will come on, the high-rise buildings glittering against the darkened sky, the neon signs flickering in coloured movement and the whole skyline brightly lit from the Battery up to Central Park. All architecture conveys a message and that of New York goes straight to the point. What matters is what you can see. The life of New York is there before you, rising into the clouds and brighter than the stars. The giants soar above all else, the Empire State and the Rockefeller Plaza, the Pan-Am Building and the Time-Life Tower. From one skyscraper IBM gives you the temperature and the time, from another there flickers the news of the day. High above all, the television masts carry their message to the world and the towering offices round Wall Street are alive with energy, insight and menace. Washington may represent a dream but New York is reality. Whatever theories may circulate, these are the facts.

There are readers of this book who will put the volume down, a few minutes from now, and shake their heads for the last time over the sordid motives which prevail in business. How much nobler, they will sigh, are those who work for the good of mankind! How much more admirable, in popular esteem, are the football players, the television personalities, the persons who cannot sing but who moan into the microphone! How degraded, by comparison, are those who work only for profit ... This is a point of view which is often expressed. But when we look at the world about us, from Vietnam to Bangladesh, from Palestine to Belfast, we discover folk with fanatical beliefs which drive them into conflict, destruction and suicide. Some will argue that belief in a real religion should teach these people how to live at peace. So it might, but a real belief in the value of money would more quickly teach them the same lesson. They would be more usefully and innocently employed in making a profit. It is the high-minded and intolerant people who do the damage, working or plotting from the highest motives. People in business, by contrast, and especially in big business, know that it is folly to quarrel with your customers or even your rivals. The essence of a business deal is normally to leave everyone satisfied; the supplier, the manufacturer, the merchant, the retailer and the customer. All have freely entered into a transaction and all have gained from it. Without a continual measure of satisfaction, trade cannot go on. A business man turned author once pointed out that freedom is the essence of business.

And then there is the clean air, the honest atmosphere of commerce; an atmosphere cleaner, brighter and more honest than any other atmosphere I know. It is almost the only department of human activity in which you can get a really clear issue, in which everything that is done is done for its own sake without ulterior motive. Such singleness of purpose is seldom possible, for example, in politics. The 'yes' or 'no' of commerce, simple, straight, understandable and honest, is hard to find in any other walk of life.[5]

In the implied comparisons between the business man and the politician, the point is that the latter, attempting to do a great deal more, may end by doing a great deal less. And the greatest danger to big business, now and in the future, arises from the contact with government: the aerospace subsidy, the defence contract, the civil servant who becomes a director, the director who ends as a politician. This is the area in which the 'clean air' of business is subject to pollution. This was true from the early days of the US railways and will be truer still as this century comes to a close.

If we are to save our civilization from tragedy, it will be through applying to politics the trained intelligence and methodical thought we have already applied to science and technology. But even that will not be enough if we fail to apply the lessons of big business: the lessons of organization and control, and above all of the international approach. No world government founded on the belief that the nations will be united can succeed. The whole idea of nationality rests upon divergent interests and mutual suspicion, sharply drawn frontiers and ill-concealed fear. Set quite apart from the blood-stained arena of nationalism is the new world of big business, a world where the jealousies of the nation states are actually forgotten. If we are to have a prosperous future we shall owe it to men who have already learnt how to co-operate and have come to see the world as one. It is an attitude we often find among mathematicians, scientists and musicians. More hopefully still, however, we find it among big business men. It is they who have the greatest lesson to teach. Are the rest of us willing to learn?

Paris, May 1968: 'Continue the struggle, capitalism is sinking.' Should big business learn from us or is it we who should learn from big business?

APPENDICES

TOP SIX COMPANIES IN SWITZERLAND 1972

Industry	Sales ($000)	Assets ($000)	Employees
1. **Nestlé** Food products.	4,130,163	3,264,347	116,034
2. **Ciba-Geigy** Pharmaceuticals, chem., dyestuffs, plastics.	2,111,962	2,645,370	71,136
3. **Brown, Boveri** Machinery, electrical equipment.	1,775,790	2,246,582	92,600
4. **Hoffmann-LaRoche** Pharmaceuticals.	1,257,120	230,221	33,000
5. **Sandoz** Pharmaceuticals, dyestuffs, chemicals.	889,151	1,077,242	32,545
6. **Sulzer** Machinery, engines.	763,910	1,073,795	37,138

TOP SIX COMPANIES IN THE NETHERLANDS 1972

Industry	Sales ($000)	Assets ($000)	Employees
1. **Royal Dutch Shell Group** Petroleum prod., natural gas, chemicals.	14,060,307	20,066,802	174,000
2. **Unilever** Food, detergents, toiletries, feed.	8,864,440	4,680,738	337,000
3. **Philips' Gloeilampenfabrieken** Electronics, elec. equip., chemicals.	6,207,009	6,857,254	371,000
4. **Akzo** Synthetic fibres, chem., pharmaceuticals.	2,565,361	2,715,064	101,000
5. **ESTEL** Iron and steel.	1,954,452	2,698,893	74,600
6. **DSM** Chemicals, fertilizers, plastics.	1,062,262	1,039,638	29,300

TOP SIX COMPANIES IN ITALY 1972

Industry	Sales ($000)	Assets ($000)	Employees
1. **Fiat** Autos, trucks, buses, tractors, engines.	3,644,732	5,674,497	189,602
2. **Montedison** Chem., synthetic fibres, pharmaceuticals.	3,597,628	5,765,252	168,000
3. **ENI** Petroleum products.	2,747,973	7,088,636	78,918
4. **Dunlop Pirelli Union** Rubber products, cables, engineering.	2,745,988	2,792,944	170,000
5. **Italsider** Iron and steel.	1,234,480	4,217,296	48,435
6. **Olivetti** Office equip., telecommunications equip.	940,131	606,414	72,273

TOP TEN COMPANIES IN JAPAN 1972

Industry	Sales ($000)	Assets ($000)	Employees
1. **Nippon Steel** Iron and steel.	5,364,332	8,622,916	98,714
2. **Hitachi** Electrical equip., appliances, machinery.	4,353,643	6,272,115	151,348
3. **Toyota Motor** Automobiles.	4,187,549	3,065,952	54,573
4. **Mitsubishi Heavy Industries** Machinery, shipbuilding, aircraft, autos.	3,980,559	7,264,272	110,563
5. **Nissan Motors** Automobiles.	3,957,557	4,767,741	81,596
6. **Matsushita Electric Industrial** Electrical and electronic equip., appliances.	3,433,771	3,195,255	82,654
7. **Tokyo Shibaura Electric** Electrical equip., appliances, electronics.	2,921,555	4,498,731	124,000
8. **Nippon Kokan** Iron and steel, shipbuilding.	2,627,727	3,770,297	47,406
9. **Sumitomo Metal Industries** Iron and steel.	2,062,470	3,968,595	41,548
10. **Kobe Steel** Iron and steel, mach., nonferrous metals.	1,901,570	3,093,041	43,010

TOP TEN COMPANIES IN GERMANY 1972

Industry	Sales ($000)	Assets ($000)	Employees
1. **Volkswagenwerk** Automobiles.	5,016,949	3,493,583	192,083
2. **Siemens** Electrical equipment, electronics.	4,712,910	4,263,094	301,000
3. **Daimler-Benz** Automobiles.	4,156,667	1,620,314	149,799
4. **Farbwerke Hoechst** Chemicals, pharmaceuticals.	4,075,712	4,651,446	146,320
5. **BASF** Chemicals.	3,719,942	3,909,541	104,045
6. **Bayer** Chemicals.	3,314,578	4,104,149	103,916
7. **AEG-Telefunken** Electrical equipment, office equipment.	3,151,424	2,305,516	166,100
8. **August Thyssen-Hutte** Iron and steel.	3,060,170	2,500,951	92,222
9. **Gutehoffnungshutte** Machinery, eng., nonferrous metals.	2,328,931	1,872,998	89,824
10. **Krupp-Konzern** Iron and steel.	2,107,640	1,892,644	74,931

TOP TEN COMPANIES IN FRANCE 1972

Industry	Sales ($000)	Assets ($000)	Employees
1. **Renault** Automobiles, tractors, machine tools.	3,536,805	1,606,104	157,000
2. **Cie Francaise des Petroles** Petroleum products.	2,806,126	3,926,075	24,000
3. **Pechiney Ugine Kuhlmann** Aluminium, chemicals, copper, special steels.	2,661,565	3,901,778	95,000
4. **Saint-Gobain-Pont-à-Mousson** Construction materials.	2,589,661	3,153,063	129,000
5. **Rhone-Poulenc** Chemicals, synthetic fibres.	2,479,281	3,326,148	118,112
6. **ELF Group** Petroleum products.	2,396,463	3,692,810	20,426
7. **Cie Générale d'Électricité** Elec. equip., telecommunications, eng.	2,163,518	3,018,949	124,500
8. **Peugeot** Autos, tools, special steels, bicycles.	2,134,194	1,517,009	90,276
9. **Citroen** Automobiles.	2,088,975	360,220	104,000
10. **Michelin** Rubber products.	1,635,574	267,862	89,000

TOP TEN JAPANESE COMPANIES 1972

Company	Sales (£M)
1. Nippon Steel Corporation	1,525.6
2. Toyota Motor Co. Ltd.	1,278.5
3. Nissan Motor Co. Ltd.	1,223.3
4. Hitachi Limited	975.4
5. Matsushita Electrical Industries Co. Ltd.	933.1
6. Mitsubishi Heavy Industries Ltd.	870.7
7. Nippon Kolan K.K.	777.5
8. Tokyo Shibaura Electric Co. Ltd.	766.4
9. Tokyo Electric Power Co. Inc.	728.3
10. Nippon Oil Co. Ltd.	650.4

TOP TWENTY AMERICAN COMPANIES 1972

Company	Sales (£000)	Capital (£000)
1. General Motors Corporation	11,331,247	4,883,987
2. Standard Oil (New Jersey)	8,425,242	6,394,203
3. Ford Motors	6,573,200	2,723,880
4. Sears, Roebuck	4,002,458	1,902,702
5. General Electric	3,770,120	1,610,960
6. Mobil Oil Corporation	3,757,005	2,539,537
7. International Business Machines	3,309,441	2,995,313
8. Texaco	3,230,920	3,711,680
9. Chrysler	3,199,736	1,318,130
10. Gulf Oil	2,948,800	3,232,800
11. International Telephone and Telegraph	2,938,312	2,223,683
12. Western Electric	2,418,806	1,402,837
13. Standard Oil of California	2,371,908	2,435,872
14. Great Atlantic and Pacific Tea	2,203,403	282,874
15. Safeway Stores	2,143,535	248,262
16. Standard Oil (Indiana)	1,986,405	1,953,044
17. United States Steel	1,971,310	2,113,117
18. Westinghouse Electric	1,852,212	1,030,210
19. Shell Oil	1,849,510	1,577,738
20. J. C. Penney	1,660,354	451,342

TOP TEN COMPANIES IN BRITAIN 1972

Industry	Sales ($000)	Assets ($000)	Employees
1. **Royal Dutch Shell Group** Petroleum prod., natural gas, chemicals	14,060,802	20,066,802	174,000
2. **Unilever** Food, detergents, toiletries, feed.	8,864,440	4,680,738	337,000
3. **British Petroleum** Petroleum products, chemicals.	5,711,555	8,161,413	70,000
4. **ICI** Chemicals.	4,236,275	5,487,041	199,000
5. **British Steel** Iron and steel.	3,630,264	3,465,700	229,000
6. **British Leyland Motor Corporation** Automobiles, trucks, buses.	3,247,877	2,085,367	190,841
7. **Dunlop Pirelli Union** Rubber products, cables, engineering.	2,745,988	2,792,944	170,000
8. **British-American Tobacco** Tobacco, paper prod., packaging, printing.	2,570,338	2,901,416	110,000
9. **National Coal Board** Coal mining.	2,537,500	1,285,775	268,000
10. **General Electric** Electrical equip., telecommunications.	2,513,719	2,848,243	166,243

TOP TEN ELECTRICS AND ELECTRONICS FIRMS 1972

Company	Country	Sales ($000)	Assets ($000)
1. General Electric (New York)	USA	10,239,500	7,401,800
2. International Business Machines (Armonk, N.Y.)	USA	9,532,593	10,792,402
3. ITT (New York)	USA	8,556,826	8,617,897
4. Western Electric (New York)	USA	6,551,183	4,309,899
5. Philips' Gloeilampenfabrieken	Netherlands	6,207,009	6,857,254
6. Westinghouse Electric (Pittsburgh)	USA	5,086,621	3,843,291
7. Siemens	Germany	4,712,910	4,263,094
8. Hitachi	Japan	4,353,643	6,272,115
9. Matsushita Electric Industrial	Japan	3,433,771	3,195,255
10. AEG-Telefunken	Germany	3,151,424	2,305,516

TOP TEN OIL COMPANIES 1972

Company	Country	Sales ($000)	Assets ($000)
1. Exon (New York)	USA	20,309,753	21,558,257
2. Royal Dutch Shell Group	Neth.-Britain	14,060,307	20,066,802
3. Mobil Oil (New York)	USA	9,166,332	9,216,713
4. Texaco (New York)	USA	8,692,991	12,032,174
5. Gulf Oil (Pittsburgh)	USA	6,243,000	9,324,000
6. Standard Oil of California (San Francisco)	USA	5,829,487	8,084,193
7. British Petroleum	Britain	5,711,555	8,161,413
8. Standard Oil (Ind.) (Chicago)	USA	4,503,372	6,186,242
9. Shell Oil (Houston)	USA	4,075,898	5,171,600
10. Continental Oil (Stamford, Conn.)	USA	3,414,984	3,249,705

TOP TEN CHEMICAL COMPANIES 1972

Company	Country	Sales ($000)	Assets ($000)
1. Unilever	Britain-Neth.	8,864,440	4,680,738
2. E. I. Du Pont de Nemours (Wilmington, Del.)	USA	4,365,900	4,283,700
3. ICI (Imperial Chemical Indus.)	Britain	4,236,275	5,487,041
4. Farbwerke Hoechst	Germany	4,075,712	4,651,446
5. BASF	Germany	3,719,942	3,909,541
6. Montedison	Italy	3,597,628	5,765,252
7. Bayer	Germany	3,314,578	4,104,149
8. Union Carbide (New York)	USA	3,261,322	3,718,342
9. Rhone-Poulenc	France	2,479,281	3,326,148
10. Dow Chemical (Midland, Mich.)	USA	2,403,709	3,312,729

TOP TEN AUTOMOBILE FIRMS 1972

Company	Country	Sales ($000)	Assets ($000)
1. General Motors (Detroit)	USA	30,435,231	18,273,382
2. Ford Motor (Dearborn, Mich.)	USA	20,194,400	11,634,000
3. Chrysler (Detroit)	USA	9,759,129	5,497,331
4. Volkswagenwerk	Germany	5,016,949	3,493,583
5. Toyota Motor	Japan	4,187,549	3,065,952
6. Daimler-Benz	Germany	4,156,667	1,620,314
7. Nissan Motors	Japan	3,957,557	4,767,741
8. Fiat	Italy	3,644,732	2,674,497
9. Renault	France	3,536,805	1,606,104
10. British Leyland Motor	Britain	3,247,877	2,085,367

TOP TWENTY AIRLINES 1972

Name	Country	Operating Revenue (£000)
1. United Airlines	USA	647,028
2. Trans World Airlines	USA	501,371
3. American Airlines	USA	498,132
4. Pan American	USA	472,280
5. Eastern Airlines	USA	421,503
6. Air France	France	268,000
7. Delta Airlines	USA	264,498
8. Japan Airlines	Japan	225,392
9. Lufthansa	W. Germany	222,184
10. Air Canada	Canada	211,809
11. Trans Australian Airways	Australia	204,296
12. British Overseas Airways Corpn.	Gt. Britain	195,532
13. Scandinavian Airlines System	Scandinavia	193,887
14. Alitalia	Italy	172,625
15. Swissair	Switzerland	153,263
16. Avianca	Columbia	151,324
17. K.L.M.	Netherlands	141,669
18. Braniff International	USA	134,974
19. British European Airways Corpn.	Gt. Britain	133,350
20. Western Airlines	USA	130,238

TOP TWENTY UK INDUSTRIAL COMPANIES 1972

Company	Main Activity	Total Turnover (£000)	Capital (£000)
1. British Petroleum	Oil Industry	3,153,300	2,026,900
2. 'Shell' Transport & Trading	Oil Industry	2,923,096	2,200,382
3. British-American Tobacco	Tobacco & Cosmetics	1,846,720	833,740
4. Imperial Chemical Industries	Chemicals, Fibres, Paints, etc.	1,524,400	1,851,800
5. Unilever Ltd.	Detergents, Margarine, Foods	1,356,800	580,900
6. Imperial Tobacco Group	Tobacco & Food	1,275,900	604,553
7. Shell-Mex & B.P.	Petroleum Distributors	1,230,000	398,000
8. British Leyland Motor Corpn.	Motor Vehicle Manufacturers	1,176,921	429,364
9. General Electrical Company	Electrical Engineers	923,649	582,201
10. Courtaulds	Man-made Fibres, Textiles, Chemicals	681,488	563,985
11. Esso Petroleum	Oil Industry	677,353	445,431
12. Ford Motor Co.	Motor Vehicle Manufacturers	588,992	293,700
13. Associated British Foods	Food Manufacturers & Bakers	585,199	160,924
14. Dunlop Holdings	Rubber Goods & Sport Requisites etc.	585,000	446,262
15. Shipping Industrial Holdings	Shipbroking & Owning Transport etc.	578,291	42,838

16. Guest, Keen & Nettlefolds	Steel & Eng. Products, Fastenings, etc.	564,840	393,220
17. Reed International	Paper, Packaging, Printing & Publishing	502,294	332,934
18. Hawker Siddley Group	Mech. Electrical & Aerospace Engineering	472,132	223,470
19. Marks & Spencer	General Store Proprietors	463,022	183,193
20. Gallagher	Tobacco	452,870	127,041

TOP TWENTY EUROPEAN COMPANIES (excluding UK) 1972

Company	Country	Main Activity	Sales 1971 (£000)
1. Royal Dutch Petroleum Company	H	Petroleum products	2,629.1
2. I.R.I.	I	State industry holding	2,655.0
3. N. V. Philips' Gloeilampenfabrieken	H	Electrical engineering, lighting, records	2,180.5
4. Volkswagenwerk A.G.	G	Motor vehicles	2,147.0
5. Unilever	H	Food products, detergents	1,712.2
6. Siemens A.G.	G	Electrical engineering electronics	1,633.1
7. Daimler-Benz A.G.	G	Motor vehicles	1,529.9
8. Farbwerke Hoechst A.G.	G	Chemicals	1,523.2
9. Nestle-Alimentana S.A.	S	Food Products	1,465.1
10. Badische Anilin & Soda-Fabrik A.G.	G	Chemicals	1,449.3
11. Bayer A.G.	G	Chemicals, pharmaceuticals	1,427.8
12. Electricite de France	F	Electricity Generating Board	1,254.7
13. August Thyssen Hutte A.G.	G	Iron, steel, chemicals	1,243.3
14. E.N.I. Group	I	Oil, chemicals, engineering, textiles	1,230.2
15. Fiat S.p.A.	I	Motor vehicles, aircraft	1,200.5
16. Allgemeine Elektrizitats-Gesellschaft AEG-Telefunken	G	Electrical engineering, electronics	1,197.8
17. Veba A.G.	G	Electricity, chemicals, glass, transport services	1,125.9
18. Pechiney-Ugine-Kuhlmann	F	Aluminium, chemicals	1,020.4
19. Cie, Francaise des Petroles	F	Petroleum products	991.7
20. AKZO N. V.	H	Man-made fibres, chemicals	969.2

NOTES

1. The Public Image

1 A.A.Berle and G.C.Means, *The Modern Corporation and Private Property* (New York 1932).
2 J.K.Galbraith, *The New Industrial State* (Boston 1967).
3 A.D.H.Kaplan, *Big Enterprise in a Competitive System*, Brookings Institute (Washington D C 1964), p. 32.

2. The Giants Emerge

1 On the oil business generally see C.Tugendhat, *Oil: the Biggest Business* (1968).
2 Excellent surveys of the pioneers of US capitalism are to be found in J.Hughes, *The Vital Few* (1966).

3. The Industrial Establishment

1 R.A.Smith, *Corporations in Crisis* (New York 1963), pp. 20–21.
2 C.Tugendhat, *The Multinationals* (1971).
3 J.Servan-Schreiber, *The American Challenge* (1967).
4 G.D.H.Cole and R.Postgate, *The Common People 1746–1946* (London 1938), pp. 638–9.
5 K.Lamott, *The Money Makers* (Boston 1969), p. 120.
6 G.Hodgson, C.Raw, B.Page, *Do you sincerely want to be rich?* (London 1971), p. 58.

4. Method and Madness

1 G.Rees, *The Multi-Millionaires* (London 1961).
2 J.K.Galbraith, *The New Industrial State* (Boston 1967).
3 Paper presented by Professor Mabel Newcomer in December 1945.
4 G.Copeman, *The Chief Executive and Business Growth* (London 1971).
5 Antony Jay, *Management and Machiavelli* (London 1967).
6 R.J.Barber, *The American Corporation: its Power, its Money, its Politics* (New York 1970), p. 64.
7 Anthony Sampson, 'The Last Tycoon', *Business Observer* (9 July 1972 et seq.).

5. Government and Unions

1 E.N.Kassalow, *Trade Unions and Industrial Relations: An International Comparison* (New York 1969), p. 22.
2 E.N.Kassalow, *Trade Unions and Industrial Relations*, p. 163.
3 T.P.Lyons, *The Personnel Function in a Changing Environment* (London 1971).
4 Robert Townsend, *Up the Organisation* (New York 1970), p. 148.
5 —— *The Development of Law on Monopoly and Competition* (1960), p. 161.
6 G.C.Allen, *The Structure of Industry in Britain*, 3rd ed. (London 1970), p. 71.
7 Allen, *The Structure of Industry in Britain*, p. 141.
8 Anthony Vice, *The Strategy of Takeovers: a Casebook of International Practice* (London 1971), p. 33.

6. The Value and Future of Big Business

1 J.Enoch Powell, *Still to Decide*, ed. John Wood (London 1971), p. 62.
2 H.J. Learitt and T.L. Whisler, 'Management in the 1980s', *Harvard Business Review* (November–December 1958).
3 Robert F. Vaudell, 'Management Evolution in the Quantative World', *Harvard Business Review* (January–February 1970).
4 Nicholas Faith, *The Infiltrators: The European Business Invasion of America* (London 1971).
5 Ernest J.P.Benn, *The Confessions of a Capitalist* (London 1925), p. 36 et seq.

ACKNOWLEDGMENTS

The pictures in this book were supplied by or reproduced by the kind permission of the following:

Atelier Populaire 14, 235; Bank of America *frontispiece*; BP 47, 49; Camera Press 10, 73, 122–3, 132, 190, 216; Carnegie Corporation 52, 53, 54; Coca-Cola 32–3, 88, 89; CBI 194; *The Director* 155; Du Pont 106–7; Esso 38–9, 42, 45; *Evening Standard* and Jak 68–9, 94–5, 110, 129, 206, 227, 229; *Financial Times* 82, 144–5; *Financial Times* and Mahood 6–7, 104, 126, 218, 232; Fisons 113; Fords 25, 58, 61, 63; John Freeman 172; General Cable Corporation 178–9; Giles and *Daily Express* 48–9; *International Management* 152–3; Krupp 22, 23; Lockheed 98, 161, 164; Nestlé 37; *The Observer* 130, 137, 152 (*below*), 212, 213; Philips, 85, 86, 87; Pirelli 90; *Punch* 9, 156, 166, 169, 185, 187 (*below*), 200; Radio Times Hulton Picture Library 11, 56, 70–1, 116, 117, 134, 181, 182, 184, 187 (*top*), 189, 205; Rowntree Mackintosh 196; Sears, Roebuck and Co 64; Toyota 79; Unesco Courier 220–1; US Embassy, London 140–1; Volkswagen 74, 75. In the appendices, tables in dollars are taken from *Fortune* magazine. Those in pounds come from *The Times* 1000.

INDEX

DATE DUE

LONDON
FOR THE GOV^R AND COMP^A OF THE BANK OF ENGLAND

J. Page

CHIEF CASHIER

£1

ONE RUPEE

ONE RUPEE

ONE RUPEE

892

REPVBBLICA ITALIANA

50

5

B₂

REPVBBLICA ITAL

500 LIRE

ITTO DI STATO A CORSO

£1

Royal Bank of Scotland Limited   A 793250
32

PROMISE TO PAY THE BEARER ON DEMAND

FIRM

ONE POUND

STERL

AT THEIR HEAD
EDINBURGH, 3
BY ORDER O

OA 712054 V   OA 7120

BANCA D'ITALIA

LIRE

MILLE

PAGABILI A VISTA AL PORTATORE

793250